CHANGE! A Student Guide to Social Action

This is the first practical social change text devoted to students working in an academic environment. While there are many books about community organizing and social change, there are no college texts focusing on how to provide real-world experience with academic content taking into consideration the flow of the academic term. *CHANGE! A Student Guide to Social Action* is written specifically for faculty and staff to use with college students with the goal of helping students bring about the change they believe is necessary to make our community a better place to live.

Dr. Scott Myers-Lipton is Professor of Sociology at San Jose State University, and is the author of *Ending Extreme Inequality: An Economic Bill of Rights Approach to Eliminate Poverty* (Paradigm 2015), *Rebuild America: Solving the Economic Crisis through Civic Works* (Paradigm 2009), and *Social Solutions to Poverty: America's Struggle to Build a Just Society* (Paradigm 2006), as well as numerous scholarly articles on racism, education, and civic engagement.

He co-founded the successful efforts to raise the minimum wage from $8 to $10 in San Jose and to modernize San Jose's business tax. He also co-founded the Gulf Coast Civic Works Campaign, an initiative to develop 100,000 prevailing-wage jobs for local and displaced workers after Hurricane Katrina. He has worked to help students develop solutions to poverty by taking them to live at homeless shelters, the Navajo and Lakota nations, the U.S. Gulf Coast, and Kingston, Jamaica. He is also on the Board of Directors for the National Jobs for All Coalition.

Scott Myers-Lipton is the recipient of the San Jose/Silicon Valley NAACP Social Justice Award, the Elbert Reed Award from the Dr. Martin Luther King Jr. Association of Santa Clara County, the Changer Maker Award from the Silicon Valley Council of Non-Profits, and the Manuel Vega Latino Empowerment Award. He lives with his wife, Diane, and his two children, Josiah and Ella, in San Jose. In addition, Scott and Diane are the proprietors of the Sequoia Retreat Center, a meeting space dedicated to individual and social transformation.

The book is very effective in part because the book is structured to align with the academic semester. Just three weeks into the semester, I can see that my students have already carried out as many actions as they accomplished all semester long last year without the book. The narrative is compelling, the examples from prior college student campaign successes are inspiring, and the focus on policy change is pushing my students to make clearer and more focused demands.

Miriam Shakow, *Associate Professor of Anthropology, The College of New Jersey*

For the past decade, the Bonner Foundation has been exploring how to develop a social action track within our network of 65 plus colleges. With the book, *CHANGE! A Student Guide to Social Action*, we now have the vehicle to help the Bonner network take this next step. Faculty on all college campuses should consider adopting *CHANGE!* so as to provide an effective and powerful social action experience for their students, and skilled civic leaders for their communities.

Robert Hackett, *President, Bonner Foundation*

CHANGE! comes at a moment in U.S. history which demands the creation of ever more powerful social and economic justice change agents, a job that higher education has done poorly. It's part roadmap, part compass, part toolkit. But above all, it's a practical guide for faculty who want to foster a new generation of able and smart activists.

Kent Glenzer, *Ph.D., Dean, Graduate School of International Studies and Management, Middlebury Institute of International Studies at Monterey*

CHANGE! A Student Guide to Social Action

Scott Myers-Lipton

Routledge
Taylor & Francis Group

NEW YORK AND LONDON

First published 2018
by Routledge
711 Third Avenue, New York, NY 10017

and by Routledge
2 Park Square, Milton Park, Abingdon, Oxon, OX14 4RN

Routledge is an imprint of the Taylor & Francis Group, an informa business

© 2018 Taylor & Francis

Library of Congress Cataloging-in-Publication Data
Names: Myers-Lipton, Scott J., author.
Title: Change! : a student guide to social action / Scott Myers-Lipton.
Description: New York, NY : Routledge, 2017. | Includes
    bibliographical references and index.
Identifiers: LCCN 2017031910 | ISBN 9781138297289
    (hb : alk. paper) | ISBN 9781138297296 (pb : alk. paper)
Subjects: LCSH: College students—Political activity. |
    Students—Political activity. | Social action.
Classification: LCC LB3610 .M94 2017 | DDC 378.1/981—dc23
LC record available at https://lccn.loc.gov/2017031910

ISBN: 978-1-138-29728-9 (hbk)
ISBN: 978-1-138-29729-6 (pbk)
ISBN: 978-1-315-09938-5 (ebk)

Typeset in Adobe Caslon and Copperplate
by Apex Covantage, LLC

This book is dedicated to all the college students who want to bring about a more democratic, equitable, and just world.

CONTENTS

STUDENT VICTORIES

- In 2007, *Students Against Sweatshops* got the San Jose State University (SJSU) president to sign an executive order creating a sweatshop-free campus.
- In 2008, *Students for EOP* led the successful campaign, along with faculty, to re-instate the SJSU Education Opportunity Program (EOP), which now serves over 2,000 first-generation, low-income students.
- In 2010, *Collective Voices for Undocumented Students* won their campaign to allow AB 540 (undocumented) students to use computers from Clark Hall and to receive certain SJSU scholarships.
- In 2011, *Students for Campus Safety* won two of their demands: (1) to have an opt-out system rather than an opt-in system for SJSU Action Alerts, and (2) to extend the SJSU shuttle service to six blocks off the campus.
- In 2012, the *Campus Alliance for Economic Justice (CAFÉ J)* developed and helped lead the San Jose Measure D campaign, which won 60% to 40% in the November election and raised the minimum wage from $8 to $10 an hour.
- In 2014, *Students for Racial Equality* led a successful campaign to remove Tower Foundation board member Wanda Ginner after she made a racist comment about Latinas.

- In 2015, *Students for DMH* won their demand for air conditioning in Dudley Moorehead Hall.
- In 2015, *College Awareness Network* won their demand for the institutionalization of a college tour program for third graders that they had developed.
- In 2015, the *Society for Teaching Responsible Options in Nutrition and Growth (STRONG)* worked with food vendors to win three changes to city regulations making it easier and more accessible for Fresh Carts to sell fresh fruit and vegetables.
- In 2016, *Spartans for a World-Class City* developed Measure G, the Modernization of the Business Tax, which won 65% to 35% in the November 2016 election and doubled the business tax by almost $13 million, focusing on mid-sized to large corporations, with the majority of the money going to fund infrastructure projects.
- In 2017, *Students Against Sexual Harassment (SASH)* won their demand to force the resignation of a professor who had sexually harassed a student, but after a two-week suspension and diversity training, had been allowed to return to his faculty position.

PREFACE

> . . . community organizing provides a way to merge various strate-
> gies for neighborhood empowerment. Organizing begins with the
> premise that (1) the problems facing inner-city communities do not
> result from a lack of effective solutions, but from a lack of power
> to implement these solutions; (2) that the only way for communi-
> ties to build long-term power is by organizing people and money
> around a common vision; and (3) that a viable organization can
> only be achieved if a broadly based indigenous leadership—and not
> one or two charismatic leaders—can knit together the diverse inter-
> ests of their local institutions.[1]
>
> Barack Obama, 1988

This book is a guide for college students to learn about the social
change ideas of community organizers, like Barack Obama, and
to utilize them within the confines of a college academic term.
This book is different than most books designed for college
students. This book not only has the student analyze a problem and develop a solution, but it also implement it. Instead
of just reading about social change, students learn about it by
actually doing it. Of course, students will still use "book knowledge," but the idea is that this knowledge will be challenged by
what is learned from social action, by developing a more critical and deeper understanding of public issues and community
change by integrating praxis with theory, while at the same time

changing social structure. Thus, this book provides an action-oriented, solutions-based experience of social change.

In this book, each chapter focuses on a different part of the process of social action, with the student learning how to turn a social problem into a social solution, and developing and implementing a campaign to achieve that solution. Importantly, the book allows students to get started on social action projects early in the semester, and then provides with the necessary tools, skills, and knowledge to run an effective campaign. In the past decade, students in my Social Action class at San Jose State University (SJSU) have used this format to run 30-plus campus, city, state, and national campaigns, and they have won 10 of them.

More specifically, the skills in this book include:

- issue development
- leadership
- recruitment
- target analysis and power mapping
- strategy and tactics
- event planning
- media outreach
- facilitation
- decision making
- fundraising
- negotiation
- evaluation

My own journey into the world of social action began in the early 1980s. I was playing professional tennis and I had achieved some success, but the life of a professional athlete was ill suited for me. It required traveling 35 weeks out of the year, which might seem fun, but is actually quite exhausting. However, professional tennis did give me the opportunity to travel around the world. It was wonderful to meet people from so many different cultures; at the same time, I saw a lot of social suffering. This led me to the decision to retire from professional tennis and to figure out what I could do to make the world a bit better place to live in.

In college, I was a political science major, so I decided to start by working for a member of congress in Northern California. I volunteered and then worked in Congressman Tom Lantos' office, and it was there that I met Edna Mitchell, the Dean of Education at Mills College, who was also the congressman's chief of staff. She suggested that I use my desire to "make a difference" and become a teacher. I told her I had never thought about being a teacher, but it sounded interesting. After checking out the program at Mills—an all-women's college but with graduate programs open to men—I decided to give teaching a shot. This lead to becoming a high school history teacher for several years, and it was in a high school classroom that my life would be changed forever.

My first job was to teach world and U.S. history at Gunn High School in Palo Alto. In one of my world history classes, I was teaching about World War II, and a freshman student asked me a question about the Holocaust. I answered her by discussing the concentration camps, the number of Jews that were killed, and the methods in which they were murdered. She interrupted me and said, "no, you don't understand my question. What I am asking is HOW could it happen?" It was then that I understood she was asking a much deeper question. She was asking how was it possible for humans to treat each other in such a barbaric and inhumane fashion. This student's question led me to search for an answer, and it changed the direction of my life.

Soon after, I left high school teaching to pursue a master's degree in the Humanities at San Francisco State, focusing on

the philosophy of Mohandas Gandhi and Dr. Martin Luther
King, Jr., I also began working at the Beyond War Foundation
as a fellow, focusing on developing non-violent methods of
resolving regional wars and nuclear war. During this fellowship,
John Anderson, a former IBM executive and Beyond War staff
member, suggested I pursue a doctorate. After reflecting on my
original question about how to make a difference, I decided to
do a Ph.D., focusing on how to bring about social change and
to create a more just and egalitarian society.

In 1989, I arrived in Boulder, Colorado, to start a doctorate
program in Sociology at the University of Colorado, as well as to
become the Assistant Director of the International and National
Voluntary Service Training (INVST) program, a project that I
developed along with Cindy Mahrer as part of the Beyond War
fellowship. After one year of working on the program design
with Dr. James Scarritt and Gaia Mika, the INVST program
accepted its first class with the goal of developing "scholar activists," who were trained to analyze and solve community and
global problems through a two-year academic curriculum that
included fall and spring service-learning projects and a domestic
and international service experience.

Service-learning, which is the integration of course concepts
and community action, was becoming popular at this time, as
academia was looking for ways to develop civically engaged students who could apply their critical thinking skills, and to make
their curriculum more relevant. In the 1990s, research confirmed
what practitioners had assumed: service-learning was effective
at making students more civically engaged, globally concerned,
less racially prejudiced, and better critical thinkers.

I continued this work in the mid 1990s, starting two more
INVST programs at Saint Mary's College of California in 1996
and San José State in 1999. However, by 2005, many of the
social problems that service-learning faculty were addressing

had worsened. In addition, I was under pressure to raise $50,000 each year to operate the SJSU INVST program. These two factors led me away from a leadership model, which focused on developing civically engaged leaders, and toward a "policy service-learning" model, which still focused on leadership, but now emphasized changing social structure.

What came out of this thinking was a semester course on "Social Action", where students develop campaigns to try to change a social policy. Now, after a decade of teaching this class on social action, I have taken the best ideas from the history of community organizing and combined them with what I have learned teaching my social action class. Using this collective knowledge, my students have won ten campaigns and have had their lives transformed. My hope is that this knowledge has the same positive results for you.

Lastly, I would like to thank my wife, Diane, and my two children, Josiah and Ella, for always inspiring and encouraging me. I would also like to thank Bobby Hackett, President of the Bonner Foundation, for his encouragement throughout the writing of this book.

Note

1 Barack Obama, "Problems and Promise in the Inner City," *Illinois Issues*, University of Illinois, Springfield, http://illinoisissues.uis.edu/archives/2008/09/whyorg.html, (accessed November 1, 2016).

A Message to the Teacher

This book is a guide for college students, but I also wrote it for you—the faculty or staff member—to have as a resource to teach college students how to do social action effectively within the confines of a college academic term. This book combines the best ideas from the history of community organizing with what I have learned from teaching my Social Action class over the past decade. Using this collective knowledge, my students have won eleven campaigns, so I know that what is in this book works. As the old saying goes, "the proof is in the pudding". I strongly believe that if you use this book, your students will also have victories, as well as transformative experiences.

What is unique about this community organizing book is that it is designed specifically for students in higher education. Importantly, it gets students into their campaigns quickly. That is why the book starts off in Chapter 1 with the selection of their campaign issue. As you know, an academic term does not provide much time (i.e., two to four months depending), so it is key that the students start their social action project as soon as possible. When I first started teaching social action, my students presented their own ideas to one another. However, as the Social Action class has become more well known, other student groups, faculty, and community organizations have asked to come in and talk to my Social Action students about joining their campaign. This might happen to you as well. Generally, there are three to five projects going on during the academic term; however, there have been a few terms when the whole class has worked on one campaign.

To ensure that your students get their campaigns up and running quickly, I recommend that the first four chapters be taught in the first three weeks of the academic term. Thus, by the end of the three weeks, you will have had your students select their issue, set their expectations, explore the key theories surrounding social action, and begin building power. As for the rest of the academic term, each chapter can take one or two weeks to complete. Upon completing Chapter 9, the students will have several more weeks of the academic term, so you may want to include another book. I have my students read *Ending Extreme Inequality*, a book that I wrote in 2012, since it introduces them to a variety of social action campaigns from a variety of perspectives. A few weeks before the end of the academic term, you will want to discuss Chapter 10 on evaluation and Chapter 11 on the hero's and shero's journey, which serves as the conclusion of the book.

This book also works well for students since it does not overwhelm them with too many things to do at once, which can often happen in a fast-moving campaign. The book asks students to perform an action and then gives them time to reflect. Many times, an "action" chapter (e.g., "Campaign Kickoff", Chapter 7) is followed by a "reflection" chapter (e.g., "Group Dynamics", Chapter 8). Thus, the book paces the action steps and offsets them with reflection, research, and critical thinking. In addition, an assignment accompanies each chapter. If you are having the students write up and turn in the assignments which is what I do—I suggest that students in each group talk about their responses to the exercises collectively, but that they write up their answers individually. This creates a good balance between group and individual work. In addition, I encourage my students to integrate the text into their assignments to demonstrate they have done the reading. Lastly, I recommend that you discuss previous social action events that have occurred at your college. For example, I tour the campus with my students to discuss the various types of social activism that have taken place on campus. As the years have passed, I have also invited former Social Action students back to campus to discuss their campaigns. This connection between former and current students provides inspiration to the latter and helps create a pipeline to careers in social action, as many of my former students continue to work for the betterment of the community in the non-profit and government sectors, and in the business world. Importantly, this course is designed to be taught every academic term, since some campaigns take three or four terms to complete. Oftentimes, the next semester's Social Action students will pick up where the previous students have left off and continue the campaign, which allows for completing campaigns that take longer than one academic term. However, whether a campaign continues or not is completely left up to the students.

Another unique aspect of the book is that it requires a different pedagogy than "teacher talk", with the professor up front and students in rows, silently taking notes. A curricular or co-curricular class on social action demands that the students are actively engaged. Thus, while I do give short lectures each time the class meets, the students also spend a good deal of time in small groups working on their group projects while I come around and help them through the challenges they are facing. In addition, when we discuss the text, I often have a few of my students facilitate the discussion so as to encourage an active role

A MESSAGE TO THE TEACHER

in the classroom. Additionally, I have my former students who have led campaigns come and talk to the students about the lessons they have learned. All of these experiences de-center me from the traditional role of teacher and ask my students to take center stage, moving them away from being receptors of knowledge to being active creators. It also begins the process of getting my students to believe that social change is possible, which many of them are fairly skeptical of. This idea of having student voices and actions at the center of the class should occur throughout the experience, which helps overcome their "schooling", which has taught them that their voice is secondary to the teacher's. My one caution is to expect a bit of chaos as the students come to terms with their power. My suggestion is to be as clear as possible about your role as "guide on the side" and to be transparent and honest with the students about your expectations. Thus, I tell my students that while they are much more in control of the class than in other college courses, I also remind them that our power is shared in that I still set the curriculum, give short lectures, provide guidance for their groups, and evaluate their work. With regards to evaluating their work, I do not give students a higher grade if they win their campaign. Rather, I evaluate their work based on the written and oral assignments.

It has been my experience that teaching social action causes concern among administrators and the larger community. When concerns have been raised, I have explained to the administration and to the press that I am teaching about democracy and exploring how power works. I assure them that what projects the students choose to work on is based on their interests and value system and that I am not coercing them into a particular project. I also remind them that the students have choice. The projects that the students select may have a liberal or conservative bent, or no bent at all (e.g., more printers for the library or air conditioning for an old building). I also tell them that there are many examples of college students working in the public realm, including business classes having students help solve problems for local companies, or engineering courses that design power grids or create software protection programs for real customers. Similarly, social action experiences provide hands-on, project-based learning opportunities that focus on democracy, power, and various forms of inequality. One other thing I tell administrators is that having students trained in social action makes the campus environment a better, more productive space to be, because without the training, it is more likely that students will be responding to the concerns they have without a full, developed plan, which can have negative consequences for the campus environment.[1]

Last of all, I will be creating an on-line discussion group for faculty and staff who are interested in sharing best practices of social action. If you are interested, please contact me at smlipton@gmail.com and I will connect you to this on-line discussion group.

Note

1 "Experiential Learning, Haworth College of Business," Western Michigan University, https://wmich.edu/business/academics/experiential (accessed April 25, 2017); Margaret Loftus, "College Engineering Programs Focus on Hands-On Learning," *US News and World Report*, September 30, 2013, www.usnews. com/education/best-colleges/articles/2013/09/30/college-engineering-programs-focus-on-hands-on-learning (accessed April 25, 2017).

1

ISSUE DEVELOPMENT

One of the highlights of the campaign is to choose what issue you are going to work on. This chapter is designed to help you choose a social action project you will work on with others in a group. Right now, you may have some general idea of what social problem you want to improve or correct. The process of choosing an issue is called issue development. Developing an issue means that you identify a solution to a social problem that you and others in your group feel strongly about and whose demand is specific, simple, and winnable, with the result of the campaign being a positive, concrete change for the community. As you are aware, the academic term is short, generally between ten to 16 weeks, so the sooner you choose an issue, the quicker you can begin to work on the campaign. To start the issue development process, it is first necessary to understand the difference between personal and social problems, and issues.

Personal and Social Problems

Most of us think in terms of *personal problems*. For example, imagine you get sick but you decide not to go to the doctor because you don't have health insurance. When the problem gets solved by either you getting better or perhaps by going to a free clinic, you might chalk up your experience to the fact that you are a student with a part-time job, and you didn't have enough money to buy health insurance. You come to the conclusion it is a personal problem, something that affects only you. If your personal problem gets solved, you may not think about it again until the next time you become sick.

There is another way to think about this same story, and that is to see it as a *social problem*. Imagine that when you become sick, you begin to talk to your roommates and class-mates about your problem, and they share with you the fact that they cannot afford health care either. Slowly, you begin to see that what you are facing is not just a personal problem affecting you, but rather a problem affecting many. And while you don't actually do anything to change society, you are now aware that what has happened to you is also happening to many others, and you now define it as a "social problem". This social problem—i.e., the inability to access health care due to cost—along with a host of other social problems, are a stan-dard feature of most undergraduate Social Problem courses in sociology, which focus on understanding the causes underly-ing them.[1]

Issue

Importantly, there is a third way to look at this same situation, and that is to see it as an *issue*. Using the framework of an issue, you would come to the same conclusion as above, but you would take the additional step of actively solving the social problem. Thus, after talking with your roommates and classmates about how they too have been unable to go to see a doctor because of a lack of health care, you decide to pull a group of students together and to demand that the university president provides financial support to cover the cost for students who cannot afford health insurance. Surprisingly, few sociology or other disciplines have courses that focus on issues. This book is written to correct this shortcoming.

As Frederick Douglass, the renowned abolitionist, once stated, "Power concedes nothing without a demand. It never did and it never will."[2] Thus, in order to create change, it is critical that a demand is made to the people in power, and this is what an issue allows for. Importantly, I am not using the word "issue" as it is normally understood as a topic of debate, but rather how it is used in the world of social action. For community organizers, an issue is a solution to the problem, which is composed of a specific demand (i.e., a concrete, measureable request) that requires a yes or no answer. The demand should be simple, stated in a single sentence, with there being a right and wrong side. A campaign has anywhere between one and three demands. A general rule in social action is to have no more than three demands, otherwise the campaign loses focus. Importantly, an issue delivers concrete, positive change in people's lives, and it should be winnable in a reasonable amount of time. In addition, you should feel strongly about an issue, as this will encourage you to put time and energy to do something about it, and make you willing to fight for it.[3]

Importantly, an issue requires a clear target, which is the lowest ranking person who can meet your demand. If the target is the city council, or a state agency, these bodies are still composed of people, and your group should identify the members that are critical for your group to convince in order to win. For example, if the city council has seven members, you will need to identify who are the four members that are the most likely to be persuaded, and target these folks. A mistake that can happen is that a group makes the demand to the wrong person. The person either doesn't have the authority to agree to the demand because it is not her or his purview, or the demand has been made too high up the chain of authority, and there is another person at a lower level that can make the decision. Of course, if the target who has the ability to make the decision denies your request, you can always go to the next level up (e.g., from the provost to the president, or from the president of the university to the chancellor of the system), but it is important to go through the correct chain of command and start with the person that has the authority to meet your demand.[4]

Many times, my students have chosen an issue because it directly affects them. For example, several of the leaders of the minimum-wage campaign were minimum-wage workers or recently had been minimum-wage workers. Similarly, the students working on air conditioning in Dudley Moorehead Hall were all students who had a class in the building. If the issue directly affects you, it means that you have a direct stake in the outcome, which generally leads to more commitment and energy for the social action project. A direct connection to the issue also allows you to be seen more easily as a stakeholder by your allies and opponents. However, it is possible to work on an issue that doesn't directly affect you. For example, my students worked with local food vendors to change a city ordinance to make it easier for the vendors to sell fresh fruit and vegetables on the sidewalk. The students were not food vendors and several of them did not live in the poorer sections of town where there were no supermarkets, but they felt passionately about the need to provide healthy food in these "food deserts".

Issue Identification

Normally, it takes several months to identify an issue to work on. This involves going out into the community to talk to people and asking them questions about what problems they are facing and what problems they think are most important. As part of this gathering of information, surveys and questionnaires are completed, and individual and small group meetings are held. After identifying what the community thinks are the major challenges it is facing, you dive deeper and ask folks such things as, "What do you mean by a 'good education'?" or "What does 'affordable health care' look like to you?" After you have uncovered what people mean when they say "good" or "affordable", you explore various solutions and test out potential demands with the community. This above process is called issue identification, and it ensures that you choose an issue that matters to the community and that it is winnable.[5]

Unfortunately, you do not have one to two months to determine an issue since the academic term is not much longer than this. If you did a normal issue identification process, the term would be over before you had the chance to actually do anything. Thus, to make the issue identification process conform to an academic term, it needs to be shortened to one to two weeks. To shorten the process, you will need to come to the next class (or meeting) with an idea for a policy change. For the purposes of this book, policy is defined as a rule, law, regulation, norm, or practice of an institution. The policy change can be on campus, or in your city, county, state, or nation. Please note that as you move to larger arenas (from campus to city to state to nation), you will need more people, power, and energy to win.

Importantly, you should put forward policy change projects that you are passionate about and are interested in. This is key since you will be working on this issue for the entire semester, so you need to be passionate about it. For a social action group to become activated, a minimum of three students must choose a policy change, since there needs to be enough people to do the group work. Three people also allows for you to learn how to work in groups, which is a democratic skill.

In preparing to decide on what issue you will be working on, please be aware that you will need to participate, which means you need to play an active role in the group discussion and be willing to share your ideas, which may involve taking risks. This may be difficult or scary, since you may be a quiet person or have not had a lot of opportunities to talk in college courses. However, social action requires that all group members participate and contribute, and while folks might take different roles in the group, everyone is expected to contribute their ideas to help the group move forward. Also, you must make a commitment to actively listen, which means that when others are talking, you are listening with your ears, but also listening by looking at facial expressions, tone of voice, and hand movements so that you really hear what the person is saying. Importantly, you will want to respond to comments in a respectful manner. Active listening will also be discussed in Chapter 8, which focuses on group dynamics.

Once you have chosen your issue as part of the below assignment, your group will want to frame the issue in the most effective way possible. A good frame for your issue expresses the values of your group, as well as connects to the shared values of your future allies and to the larger public. For example, conservative organizations have used the frame of "family values" or "pro-life" when arguing for various restrictions to abortion, while liberal organizations have used the frame of "fairness" and "self-sufficiency" to increase the minimum wage. The frame that your group selects will be used on posters and in press releases, and it will be repeated over and over by your group members, and it will shape your organizational rap (discussed in Chapter 4) and campaign message (discussed in Chapter 7).[6]

Case Studies

Over the past decade, my students in Social Action have used this issue development process to win eleven campaigns. All of their policy changes started with the same process described above, so this should give you some confidence that what you are about to go through will work and be meaningful. Of course, my students have lost some of the campaigns they have created, but whether they have won or lost, they have all gone through this same process. Let's discuss five of these campaigns, with a focus on how their issues were developed and framed.

In the fall of 2011, Natasha Bradley, an SJSU student, began to become nervous about her safety. That academic year, there had been a murder in one of the campus garages, and the students on campus were not informed by the campus police for several hours about what had taken place. At the same time, there had been two sexual assault cases reported near the campus. Natasha had originally joined a social action group focusing on increasing the African American graduation rate, but she was so passionate about this social problem that she convinced her group of six students to switch their focus to campus safety. They named their group *Students for Campus Safety*.

Students for Campus Safety decided on the following policy changes: (1) the University Police Department (UPD), which oversaw the evening escort program, should increase its service from one to six blocks surrounding the campus; (2) the university should change their Alert SJSU system to automatically send alerts to all campus members, even if they have not signed up; and (3) the UPD should increase the number of campus blue light call boxes, which provide remote locations with access to the police. In addition, *Students for Campus Safety* chose their target, the UPD police chief, and they focused all their actions on him. Notice that the first two demands were very specific, while the third policy change could have been more specific if the group had stated how many blue lights they wanted to increase. Specificity is important so the target knows what he is saying yes or no to. Furthermore, specificity (i.e., in this case, a quantitative number) allows the group to estimate the cost of the proposed policy changes. Within the year, *Students for Campus Safety* would go on to win all three of their demands.

Reflecting back on the campaign, Natasha, one of the key student leaders, stated:

> Originally our group wanted to address the graduation rate of Latino and African-American males at San José State but once safety on the campus became an issue, we immediately changed it. At the time of the project, I was already in my last year of school so I had already been familiar enough with the campus and the surrounding city that walking around alone was never an issue. But for the first time, walking to the bus stop scared me because I thought that something was going to happen to me. So when the opportunity arose to make myself and other students feel safer, I jumped at the opportunity. During the fall semester in 2011, there were a combination of sexual assaults and robberies that took place within a short period of time both on and off campus, leaving many students, like myself, feeling unsafe even walking around campus at night. Our group wanted to implement three ways to create a safer campus for students, staff, and faculty. What I learned about from the campaign is that social change is actually possible. When people care enough about an issue and there's enough people from different sectors, then a lot can be accomplished and can be accomplished quickly.

Notice Natasha's passion about the issue, her personal connection to the issue (which helped to maintain her motivation), the group's use of three demands, and how this social action project convinced her that social change is possible.

In the fall of 2013, Professor Maria Luisa Alaniz, a faculty member from the Department of Sociology and Interdisciplinary

Social Sciences, came into the Social Action course on the second day of class, when the students were beginning the process of choosing their issue, to ask for help on a campaign she was involved with. After five years of doing this course, this was quite a common practice, as faculty and community members were aware that Social Action students would choose their projects early in the semester, and since the students had been successful previously, they began asking if they could come into class to present their policy change and to ask the students to join them. Dr. Alaniz informed the students that a member of the SJSU Tower Foundation, the university's fundraising unit, had made a blatantly racist comment, stating "I contribute to this University because these little Latinas do not have the DNA to be successful." She noted that a university vice president, and member of the President's Cabinet, was present at the meeting and remained silent. This was particularly shocking since San Jose State had a "See Something, Hear Something, Say Something" campaign against racism in response to a recent hate crime on campus.

Dr. Alaniz informed the students that a Latina staff member, who was also present at the meeting, had made an informal complaint, but no action was taken. She encouraged the staff member to make a formal complaint, which she did. However, Dr. Alaniz was worried that no action would be taken unless more pressure was brought to bear upon the campus administration, particularly the president. Thus, she asked the students to become involved to help remove the member of the SJSU Tower Foundation who made the racist comment. Out of a class of 35, 14 students (13 Latinos and one African American) decided to join this campaign.

The 14 students felt strongly about this issue, were willing to put in time and energy to do something about it, and were willing to fight for it. In response, the students created *Students for Racial Equality*, and they developed three demands: (1) the removal of the Tower Foundation board member, (2) a letter of apology from the university to the Latina staff member who was present at the meeting and made the formal complaint, and (3) mandatory anti-racism trainings for administration, faculty, staff, and students. *Students for Racial Equality* targeted the university president, and all actions were focused on him. Within three days of the group's kickoff event, the president was pushed to act, with the president announcing that the board member was stepping down. At this time, the president also announced the resignation of the vice president who was present at the meeting but did not challenge the racist comment. Within the year, the second demand was met, as the president apologized in a letter to the Latina staff member who had filed the informal and formal complaint.

Once again, the issue directly affected the students since they had personally felt the negative impacts of racism. In addition, as members of the campus community, students had a direct stake in making the campus community an open and welcoming space for all students. This direct connection with the issue can be seen in the words of Estelia Velasquez, one of the main student leaders for *Students for Racial Equality*, when she stated:

> What motivated me to become involved with *Students for Racial Equality* was the issue that we were presented with. When Dr. Alaniz came and spoke to the class about the racist comment that was made during a Tower Foundation board meeting, I was appalled that someone who donates to the University believes that Latinas do not have the DNA to be successful. And the fact that the University was taking so long in addressing the issue made me angry and made me think that making racist remarks towards Latino/a's was acceptable when it is not. This motivated me

because as a Latina. I do have the DNA to be successful and I wanted to show the University that we do matter and that they need to work differently in how they work out these issues.

Again, Estelia was incredibly passionate about the issue because it directly affected her. While it is not necessary to have a direct connection with the issue, it does help with motivation and allows for you to speak to the issue personally.

A third case study is from 2010, when a group of students created the *Campus Alliance for Economic Justice (CAFÉ J)* and developed a policy change to raise the minimum wage in San Jose from $8 to $10. Marisela Castro—the daughter of farmworkers—came up with the idea for raising San Jose's minimum wage. At the time, Marisela was working at an afterschool program, and it was there that she saw kids taking snacks and putting them into their backpacks. When Marisela talked to the kids about why they were taking food, the students disclosed that they did this because they didn't have enough food at home, and their brothers and sisters were hungry. Marisela asked them if their father and mother were working, and the kids told her that both of them were working, and their dad was working two jobs, but they were at minimum wage, so there wasn't enough money to buy food sometimes. Marisela was outraged. After telling me this story in my Wealth, Poverty and Privilege course, she looked at me and said, "Profe, we have to do something. This can't continue for another generation!" In the course, the students had read about raising the minimum wage at the local level, and after class, she came up to me to discuss the possibility of doing this in San Jose. I told her that there was no action component in the Wealth, Poverty and Privilege course, but there was an action component in Social Action, and that she should considering taking it the following semester, which she did.

At the beginning of the next semester, Marisela presented her idea of raising the minimum wage, and three students from the class joined her. After several meetings, these four students decided to put forward a city ballot measure to be voted on by the people to raise the minimum wage from $8 to $10. Their main target was the voting population in San Jose, with a secondary target being the city council, since they had the power to put the measure on the ballot without having to collect the almost 20,000 signatures, which was what eventually happened. Hundreds of meetings later, and with students from three consecutive Social Action classes working on this issue, and with the help of their allies in the labor, faith, and non-profit communities, San Jose voted 60% to 40% in November of 2012 to enact one of the largest one-time minimum-wage increases in the history of the nation.

Once again, the issue directly affected the students. Eighty percent of the students at San Jose State work, and about one-quarter of them make minimum wage, with many more making just above minimum wage. In addition, the students became a major stakeholder and worked closely with the other stakeholders (i.e., unions, non-profit organizations, and the faith community) to win this campaign. One of the key organizers of the campaign, Elisha St. Laurent, was a single mom who had been a minimum-wage worker. Yet, soon after she began to work on this issue, she became aware of how hard it is to bring about social change and to win a campaign. She began to lose interest in the campaign and began thinking it was only important because it was a class project. However, Elisha was then asked to speak at an event about her experience being a single mom and living on a minimum-wage job. This changed everything. After this event, she began to feel more connected to the issue and more motivated to work on the campaign. Elisha went on to become one of the key leaders of the minimum-wage victory, which goes to show that if a group provides its members with meaningful action, it leads to individual transformation. At the same time, if the group does not provide its members with meaningful action, students lose interest, and the group becomes less effective.

A fourth case study is from the fall of 2006, when, on a cold November evening, a group of 40 SJSU students slept out on campus to show solidarity with the poor and homeless. A report had been released showing that Silicon Valley was now the "homeless capital" of Northern California, with 7,600 people without housing on any given night. The students responded to this report by calling for a campus sleep out they entitled "Poverty Under the Stars" to demonstrate their solidarity with the poor, an event that they have continued each November up to the present day.

As part of the sleep out, the students watched *When the Levees Broke* by Spike Lee, a movie that had just been released showing how over 1,830 died, 250,000 houses were destroyed, and 500,000 people were displaced because of Hurricane Katrina. The students were deeply moved by the social suffering they saw and were outraged to learn that the public infrastructure had not been properly maintained, that the immediate response from the government had been shamefully slow, and that the rebuilding had taken too long.

After the students woke up, we got breakfast and went to class. That morning, I happened to be teaching about how unemployment was reduced from 23% to 10% as part of the New Deal programs. I went on to discuss how President Roosevelt created the Civil Works Administration in 1933 with an Executive Order and that, within two months, 4.2 million Americans were hired to do public works (e.g., school repair, sanitation work, and road building). The students and I saw the connection between FDR's public works program and what we had seen the previous night, and we began to formulate a solution: hire Gulf Coast residents at living wages and rebuild their public infrastructure. We named the project the *Gulf Coast Civic Works Project* (GCCWP).

The next step was to reach out to Gulf Coast organizations to understand if this was something that they might support. The students and I wrote many non-profit organizations involved in the rebuilding, and we received a very enthusiastic response. Then, 100 students from around the country traveled to Louisiana and Mississippi to talk first-hand with the communities most impacted by the damage, and after conducting hundreds of interviews with Gulf Coast residents, the students outlined four demands, which were included in the federal legislation that became known as House Resolution 4048: The Gulf Coast Civic Works Act. The demands, which were based on what they had heard from the community, were: (1) create 100,000 public works jobs at prevailing-wage jobs (2) if workers do not have these skills, paid apprenticeships should be provided; (3) the local communities affected by Hurricane Katrina should decide which structures would be given priority to rebuild; and (4) the process to obtain a civic works job should be simple, with a streamlined process conducted at county employment service offices or through faith-based and community initiatives connected to the White House.

Interestingly, many of the Social Action students didn't have a direct connection to the Gulf Coast, but they did understand right from wrong. Eric A., one of the GCCWP members, reflected on why he was motivated to become involved in this social action project, stating:

> I was drawn by the horrific reality for such a great amount of people in our community, and the strategic hope for a better future. As time went on, I became totally focused

on the need for action. After learning about what was happening in the Gulf Coast, there was just no way I could do nothing and pretend everything was okay. Someone had to do something—why not me, us? As my first major involvement in community organizing, I learned an immense amount about what it took to work together in realizing real social change.

Thus, Eric and many other students became involved in an issue that was far away from their home because they felt an obligation to right a wrong. Also, note that like many college students in a social action class, this was Eric's first experience doing social change.

Lastly, in the spring of 2015, a representative from Sacred Heart Community Services, the largest anti-poverty organization in Silicon Valley, came into my Social Action class on the second day of instruction and presented to the class the opportunity to help them organize food vendors who were selling uncut fruits and vegetables. The local food vendors had banded together to demand a change in a city ordinance to allow for: (1) an increase in the number of hours from two to eight that a mobile cart vendor can vend on private property, with the permission of the landlord; (2) a decrease in the buffer from 100 feet to 50 feet between a "Fresh Cart" vendor and residential property; and (3) permission to vend on government sites including post offices and California DMVs. Four students agreed to join the effort to support the "Fresh Cart" vendors, with the students naming their group *STRONG* or *Society for Teaching Responsible Options in Nutrition and Growth*. Students from three successive Social Action classes worked on this issue with the food vendors, and all three demands were won.

As with the Gulf Coast Civic Works Project, the *STRONG* students were not directly affected by this issue. They were not food vendors, nor did they live in the areas where there were food deserts. However, they were motivated by a sense of justice and were excited about supporting the food vendors in the efforts to change city policy. In this campaign, the students played a supportive role. Sacred Heart provided an organizer for the campaign, and the students went to many meetings with the food vendors. At the food vendor meetings, the students listened carefully and provided insights into strategy and tactics when appropriate, helped with the publicity for a public event, helped organize a letter-writing campaign to city council members, and mobilized students and community members to attend the city council meeting when the issue came before it. Interestingly, the students obtained a meeting with a city council member who was not interested in meeting with the food vendors, but when the students asked him for the meeting, he readily agreed. The Sacred Heart organizer commented that the meeting would not have happened without the students' involvement. The students were glad that they could get this meeting with the city council member, but they were also aware that it was due to their privilege as students. Ultimately, the students were okay with it, since they saw themselves working with the food vendors and were not doing things for them.

Assignment

After learning about issue development, spend some time reflecting on a policy you would like to work on. At the next class or meeting, you will have three to five minutes to present your policy change idea. The policy change should have one to three specific demands or asks. In addition, students from the previous semester's Social Action campaigns, other student groups, faculty and staff, and community groups may be invited to this meeting to present their policy change ideas. If an idea is presented as a problem (e.g., there are too many homeless people in our community), or as a slogan (e.g., we need more living-wage jobs), brainstorm together to make it an issue (i.e., a solution with a specific demand and a target, etc.).

Following the presentations, you should break into the group that you would like to join to discuss further the policy change, as well as to do introductions, provide contact information to each other, and discuss why this issue is of interest. Remember, you need a total of three students to make a group. Please know that these are not the final groups, and you may want to move to another group in the next few weeks, or even in the middle of the semester if for some reason your group is not working out. If you did not find two other students to join in a group, and there are other students in the same situation, work with the professor or staff member over the next week and work to find an issue you can agree upon. If there are not two other students in the same situation, you will need to join one of the other groups.

After you have broken into groups, please respond to the following questions, as they will help create an issue that has a specific demand that can be directed at a target. Remember, good issues are specific, simple, winnable, and deliver concrete, positive change.

1.1   What is the social problem that your group will work on?
1.2   What is the policy your group wants to change? Please provide one to three demands.
1.3   Who is the target?
1.4   Do you feel strongly about your issue? Are you willing to fight for it?
1.5   How will your group's solution provide positive change in people's lives?

1.6   What is the best "frame" for your issue?

1.7   Testing your demands/issue: As part of your issue identification, go out and interview two to three students
and ask them the following: How concerned are you
about your issue? How does the issue impact you (or
not)? Do you agree with the demands? Would you be
willing to work on this issue, and fight for it? Please
record their answers and include a description of the
people you interviewed (e.g., age, year in school, lives
on/off campus, gender, ethnicity/race). Importantly,
analyze their responses, and explain what are the
implications of their responses for your campaign. For
example, if the interviewees are unconcerned about the
issue or unwilling to fight for it, your group may need
to change the message, the demand, or perhaps even
the issue itself. In your responses, integrate course readings and ideas discussed in the text with your answers.

1.8   Testing your demands/issue: In teams of two or
three, go out and talk to various stakeholders (e.g.,
the student body president, a rabbi or minister, the
director of a non-profit, a union leader, etc.) that
focus on your issue. Ask her/him: Are you addressing your social problem? If so, how? Then tell them
how your group is conceptualizing the issue and ask
them if they think this approach makes sense. Do
they agree with your approach? If so, why, and if not,
why not? Also, ask whether, if your group moves forward, they would support you or become involved as
an ally. If so, what would they be willing to do? In
addition, ask them who else is working on solving
this social problem, and whether they can connect
you to them. Who else should you talk to? Lastly,
ask them if they have any questions for you. In your
responses, integrate the text with your answers.

1.9   Begin keeping track of the hours you work in the
      community. At SJSU, students do a minimum of 25
      hours of community work for the semester.

Notes

1   Joan Minieri and Paul Gestos, *Tools for Radical Democracy: How to Organize for Power in Your Community* (San Francisco: Jossey-Bass, 2007).
2   Frederick Douglas, "West India Emancipation," *University of Rochester Frederick Douglass Project*, http://rbscp.lib.rochester.edu/4398 (accessed September 19, 2017).
3   Minieri and Gestos, *Tools for Radical Democracy*; Si Kahn, *Organizing: A Guide for Grassroots Leaders* (Silver Spring, MD: NASW Press, 1991); Rinku Sen, *Stir It Up: Lessons in Community Organizing* (San Francisco, CA: Jossey-Bass, 2003).
4   Minieri and Gestos, *Tools for Radical Democracy*.
5   Minieri and Gestos, *Tools for Radical Democracy*; Sen, *Stir It Up*.
6   Sen, *Stir It Up*.

2

SETTING THE TONE

In this opening week of the academic term, it is extremely important to set the right tone for the journey ahead. To set the right tone for your campaign, the first topic that must be addressed is whether you believe that social change is even possible. I have come to learn that many of my students, deep down, don't believe that social change is possible. They might give lip service to it, and they might even cite the suffragette movement or the civil rights movement as an example that change is possible. However, many students don't believe that *they* can bring about social change. This is not surprising to me since most major decisions in the public sphere seem to be in the hands of others, and they are given little opportunity to help make decisions that affect society. Furthermore, their high school and college experience, and perhaps your experience, have led them (and maybe you) to believe that your voice doesn't matter, since many classrooms are filled with "teacher talk", with the teacher or professor up front and the students in rows, taking notes silently. However, social action is about democracy, so you will be expected to engage and participate actively. In order to set the right tone, be aware that from the very beginning of this social action experience you will be expected to participate actively.

Redefining Leadership: Seeing Yourself as a Leader

You will be called upon to be a leader in this social action project. However, the problem is that you might not see yourself as a leader. This is the result of a narrow definition of leadership, which assumes that leaders are people who are charismatic, dynamic, visionary, and powerful. In this definition, leaders are people who stand up and give an inspirational speech or take control in a situation, and they make something happen. These leaders are always out in front, leading the pack. Unfortunately, this type of leadership excludes many people who are more quiet and reserved or don't see themselves as public speakers or visionary, and it oftentimes disempowers people in the group, since if they don't fit this description of a leader, they conclude that they must be followers.

A more inclusive and empowering definition of leadership is needed if we are to get more people engaged in solving social problems. I believe that leadership should be defined as someone who thinks about the group and helps it function effectively. This definition of leadership allows for all of us to become leaders and is not based in having more influence or power in the group. To become a leader, what we need to do is to spend time thinking about what are the needs of the group and to put forward creative solutions to the problems that the group is facing. In other words, the person is a leader if she takes responsibility for the group.[1]

In your social action campaign, you will have many opportunities to take leadership in this non-oppressive fashion. In your group, there will be many problems to solve: everything from how the group functions, to how your group recruits new members, to how the group works with the media. All these problems will take the best thinking of the group members. The goal is to get as many people involved in coming up with solutions to these group problems as possible. In a campaign, there are hundreds of details to consider and to do, so it needs all group members to contribute in order to be successful. Of course, there is an action component to this definition of leadership, but with more people involved in the group process, it opens up the possibility for more people to engage in the more traditional leadership activities, like giving a speech or leading a march.

Below are some qualities and skills that you may want to consider developing so that you can effectively contribute to your group. You may have been born with them, or you may have developed them as a result of your family life or through sports. Whatever the case, you should be aware that these leadership qualities exist, and they can help you and your group to be effective. These qualities include:

- **Becoming a good listener**
  Earlier models of leadership focus on the great communicator, whether that be President Ronald Reagan or Dr. Martin Luther King, Jr. However, Cesar Chavez, the co-founder and organizer for the United Farm Workers (UFW), reminds us that it is necessary to be a good listener. Cesar spent a great deal of time listening to his fellow farmworkers, realizing that it was important to hear their ideas and stories if they were to achieve the UFW goal to negotiate with businesses through collective bargaining. At one meeting, when it was unclear how to move forward, and Cesar admitted he had no good response, it was the voice of an elderly female farmworker who provided the answer on what the next step of the campaign should be. She started by saying, "Well, I know I am not qualified, but there was something. I had an idea, maybe just a small idea, but maybe it can help," and she went on to describe that since the UFW had been barred from

organizing at the farmworker camps where the workers lived, they should create a small church on the public roadway across from the camps to attract the workers to come and visit. Cesar and the UFW listened, and they decided to do exactly as this "unqualified" elderly farmworker suggested. Thus, it is critical that we listen to all in the group. It is also important to ask good questions, such as: "What are your thoughts?", "How does it make you feel?", and "What if . . . ?" These open-ended questions will allow you to hear from people what they are thinking and feeling.[2]

- **Becoming comfortable talking in a small group and in public**
  Learning to speak in a small group and in public doesn't mean you have to be the person to deliver the major address at an event or speak all the time in the group. However, it does mean that when the opportunity presents itself, you are able to communicate to others effectively. Thus, if someone asks you about the campaign, whether it be a fellow student in a class, the president of the university, or the press, you must learn to articulate clearly what the campaign is about. It is not necessary for all group members to be dynamic speakers, but everyone should be able to explain what is the demand, who is the target, how will the solution make our community better, and what motivated them to be involved in the campaign. In addition, all people should be comfortable speaking to the group about their concerns and issues.

- **Becoming aware of how the group is "feeling"**
  A major part of whether your group is successful is how the group works together. If members feel good about the working relationships in the group, there is a much higher chance of being successful. Thus, it is very important to become aware of the group dynamics. Is the group feeling good about

how they are working together, or is there discontentment? Do members have negative feelings about the group that are not being talked about? Are people frustrated that some people are doing more work than others or that some people are dominating the discussion? Are people sharing power? If you see that the group is not working well together, you need to take responsibility to talk to the people that have these feelings, and see if it can be worked out individually, or perhaps in the larger group.[3]

- **Having integrity**
  Be honest in all of your dealings with the group. In addition, don't say anything about group members that you would not say to their face. Lastly, if you say you are going to do something, make sure it gets done. This ability to accomplish what you say you are going to do helps the group immensely. So if you tell people you are going to do something, do it. If for some reason you can't get it done, tell the group, and ask for help to get it done.

- **Understanding how privilege operates and learning to work with groups who are "different" than you**
  Society provides more or less status and privilege to people based on race, gender, social class, sexual orientation, educational attainment, immigration status, and religious affiliation. The more you learn about yourself and your own identity and privileges (or lack thereof), as well as the identity and privileges of others, the better. This understanding of privilege, and its intersectionality, will help you to better understand the dynamics of the group, as well as the relationships between the group and your allies.

- **Being persistent**
  Persistence is perhaps one of the most important qualities of being a leader. The most effective leaders are the ones who, when they wake up in the morning, think about what they

can do today to move the campaign forward, and when they go to bed at night, think about what they can do tomorrow. To be a leader, there is a certain level of stick-to-it-iveness that is absolutely critical.

- **Learning to say "no"**
  If you have the above qualities and skills, or are developing them, people from other groups will see that you are a "leader" and will ask you to become involved in their issues. While this may be flattering, learn to say "no" with a smile. You do not want to get into a situation where you take on too many things and become burned out. Learn to say, with a smile, "Thank you so much for that invitation to work on this project, but I am focused on this campaign right now."

In addition, this book provides the opportunity to develop some specific skills. These skills are highly valued in society, and they will help you get a job in the non-profit, public, or private sectors. These skills include how to:

- Facilitate a meeting
- Conduct research
- Recruit members
- Work with the media
- Work in a group effectively
- Plan events for an entire campaign
- Fundraise
- Confront and negotiate with a target
- Evaluate your project

In your social action campaign, you will have the opportunity to practice and develop these skills. Some of these skills may be more appealing to you than others, and it will be up to you to decide which skills you may want to develop.

Plato's Cave

Twenty-three hundred years ago, Plato, the Greek philosopher, wrote the Allegory of the Cave (see: http://webspace.ship. edu/cgboer/platoscave.html). In Plato's Cave, he imagines that a group of people have been chained down from birth and are unable to move their heads to see behind them, where there is a fire throwing up images of objects on the cave's wall in front of the prisoners. The chained-down people think these objects are real and alive, as they are not aware that they are shadows of objects. However, a person breaks free, turns around, and becomes aware of the reality of the situation. At the top of the cave there is an opening, and the person ascends out of it. Upon exiting the cave, the person is bathed in the light of the sun (i.e., wisdom) and is able to see reality clearly. Soon after, the person returns to the cave to inform the people about what was observed.

Plato's Cave provides insight into whether humans are truly free, who is controlling society (and its images) and for what purpose, what is the process to liberate our minds, and what will happen to us once our minds are liberated and we engage with others in society. As you begin your social action project, reflecting on these insights will be extremely helpful as you set the right tone for you and your group.

Assignment

The below questions start the process of moving you away from being a receptor of knowledge to being an active creator, and moving the professor or staff away from being a sage on the stage to being a guide on the side that facilitates your learning process. The first set of questions focuses on your thoughts about social change. In your responses, please integrate the text with your answers:

2.1 What do you know about social change?

2.2 How does social change take place?

2.3   Why would someone become involved in social change?

2.4   Do you believe that social change is possible?

Please analyze the following questions about Plato's Allegory of the Cave:

2.5   What do the fire, shadows, and cave represent?

2.6   What does the ascent out of the cave represent?

2.7   What happens to people who decide to go back into the cave?

2.8   How might service-learning, which is the integration of civic action and academic concepts, help us to get of the cave?

2.9   How does Plato's Cave apply to us today?

In your group, please reflect on the following questions about leadership:

2.10 What are your thoughts about the traditional and the new definition of leadership described above? When you think of traditional leadership, what are the images that come to mind?

2.11 In previous group experiences, how has "leadership" played out? Has leadership been shared and has everyone had the opportunity to exercise leadership? How have you had to deal with people not taking responsibility for the group and relying on others, or the opposite, where a person has been too dominant?

2.12 Which are your strongest and weakest leadership qualities and skills, as described above? What quality and skill would you like to develop in this campaign?

2.13 How will your group make sure that you have shared leadership and that all are contributing their ideas and actions?

Notes

1 Rocky Mountain Peace Center, *Communities of Conversation and Action, a Manual for Building Community* (Boulder, CO: Rocky Mountain Peace Center, 1988).
2 Juanita Brown, "A Single Voice," UC San Diego Library, https://libraries.ucsd.edu/farmworkermovement/essays/.../028%20Brown_Juanita.pdf (accessed March 20, 2017).
3 Rocky Mountain Peace Center, *Communities of Conversation and Action.*

3

CHANGE THEORY

By the second week of the campaign, you have joined a group with at least two other students to work on an issue, and you have been discussing leadership and setting the "right tone" for your group. It is now time to reflect on the different theories of social change. In the previous chapter, you were also asked to discuss how social change takes place and whether you thought it was possible. Importantly, there is an entire literature examining the dynamics of social change. This chapter explores this literature, with a focus on the general categories that explain macro social change, the role of groups in creating community change, and how critical education theory explains change and service-learning.

Macro Change

On the wall of the Vatican Palace is Raphael's fresco *The School of Athens*, which depicts the most renowned Greek, Arab, Roman, and Persian thinkers all in the same time and space engaged in multiple conversations. At the center of the fresco is Aristotle and Plato, with the former holding his hand out and flat, and the latter holding his hand up and pointing his index finger to the sky. Scholars have interpreted this to mean that Aristotle is suggesting that ultimate reality lies in the material world, where Plato finds ultimate reality to be in the realm of ideas.

Raphael's depiction of where ultimate reality lies connects to the two general categories that explain large-scale, macro social change, since one category focuses on materialistic reasons (i.e., economic production and technology), while the other category focuses on idealistic factors (i.e., ideas, beliefs, and values). A materialist perspective believes that the modes of economic production and technology shape and create the social organization and the social relations of production (e.g., between capitalist and factory worker), as well as the values and norms of a society. One of the most famous materialist thinkers is Karl Marx, who summarized this perspective by stating "the windmill gives you a society with the feudal lord, the steam-mill the society with the industrial capitalist."[1] For a materialist, social change occurs when economic production or technology changes. Accordingly, Marx maintained that when the factory replaced the windmill as the main production technology, it caused society's ideology, values, and norms to change, as well as the social organizations (e.g., political structures). The feudal system, with its focus on authority coming from the king through the lords, which both controlled the serf, was overthrown by the factory system, which was supported by small- and large-scale capitalists who put forward new political structures (i.e., representative democracy) and promoted new ideologies based on political freedom and new values based on meritocracy. These materialist factors are at the heart of Marxism and conflict theory, which both focus on how power is used by the economic elite to dominate and reproduce the existing social systems (e.g., political, economic, education, and family).

The other category that explains large-scale, macro social change focuses on idealistic factors, such as beliefs, values, and ideology, as the main cause. Ideationalists argue that there are three ways that ideas promote macro social change: (1) ideas point out the contradictions, discrepancies, and problems within a society; (2) ideas provide legitimacy to a preferred course of action; and (3) ideas offer the necessary social solidarity to bring about change. Consequently, an ideationalist maintains that the rise of the factory system and industrial capitalism was the result of the Protestant value system— specifically Calvinism—which supported hard work, worldly achievement, and frugality. This Protestant value system provided legitimacy to capitalism and provided the necessary social solidarity to overthrow the feudalistic system. One of the most famous ideationalist thinkers was Max Weber, who argued that "the spirit of capitalism" played a leading role in the change from feudal lords to the industrial capitalist. Weber believed that Calvinism's

> religious valuation of restless, continuous, systematic work in a worldly calling, as the highest means to asceticism, and at the same time the surest and most evident proof of rebirth and genuine faith, must have been the most powerful conceivable lever for the expansion of that attitude toward life which we have here called the spirit of capitalism.

For the ideationalist, it was this belief in the sanctity of work, worldly achievement, and frugality that provided the necessary conditions for capitalism to develop. Later in his life, Weber acknowledged that both idealist and material factors worked together to lead to the rise of capitalism in the West, stating that "not ideas, but material and ideal interests, directly govern men's conduct." Weber was making sure that ideationalist factors were included in discussing social change, and that change was not solely a result of materialist factors.[2]

Assignment

The below assignment provides you with the opportunity to integrate theory and practice (i.e., your campaign). With this in mind, please answer the following questions:

3.1 How have materialist and ideationalist factors affected your issue?

3.2 How do idealistic factors, with its focus on beliefs, values and ideology, connect to how you are framing your issue?

3.3 How might this knowledge of materialist and idealistic factors help your group win the campaign?

Community Change

The materialist and ideationalist explanations of social change operate at the large-scale, macro level and leave little room for change initiated by small groups at the community level. This local level of change has been much less studied; however, there is a growing body of literature focusing on local change brought about by groups. The two major models focusing on community change are the women-centered model and Saul Alinsky's model of organizing. Both models attempt to bring about social change by individuals forming groups and working to change the social system, and both models have had a significant impact on the development of the United States. This book utilizes the women-centered approach to group dynamics and Alinsky's understanding of power.

Women-Centered Model

There are two main sources of the women-centered model of organizing for community change. First, predominantly white women working in the late 19th and 20th centuries expanded their concern for their homes and families, and extended it into the public sphere, where they worked on improving their city services, education, housing, health care, and labor laws. A women-centered model of organizing takes this caring and nurturing of people—generally seen as in the private sphere—and expands it to the public sphere, with women becoming "activist mothers" who are concerned not just with their children, but with all the children in the community. This connection to others leads to a value system that focuses on the community rather than individual self-interest. It can also focus on the process of empowerment as the key to community organizing rather than building power, with relationships being the key to sustain the struggle over time. Importantly, this ethic of care is not biologically derived as women's "natural role", but rather it is socially constructed from American norms and values that have promoted women taking care of the family.[3]

The goal is to bring people together to resolve conflict and build community. This work is done in small groups and is highly relational, where trust can build and listening can take place. Women-centered organizing provides a safe space for community members to grow and develop, and it emphasizes the importance of building a safe space where they develop the belief that it is possible to work for the betterment of others and themselves, rather than initially focusing on changing policies or institutional structures. In a women-centered organizing model, the people that organize and the people that lead are many times the same folks. In addition, this model focuses on encouraging the development of many leaders, and can be said to be group-centered, rather than developing an individual leader or two that speaks for the group.

The earliest version of the women-centered model is the settlement house movement of the late 19th century. In 1884, the first settlement house was developed in east London, and a few years later, the first settlement house in the United States was

developed; by 1910, there were 400 settlement houses oper-
ating in the nation. Settlement houses were social centers for
civic engagement. The people that lived in these communal set-
tings were young, white, and college-educated. The residents
lived in poor urban neighborhoods, where they would live for
about three years. The residents lived with the marginalized
because they believed that there was too large of a gap between
the rich and poor, and that in order to maintain social cohe-
sion, there needed to be interaction between the social classes.
Importantly, the residents did not come up with solutions for
the community, but rather, the solutions developed from the
needs and desires of the poor. Initially, the settlement houses
worked on education (e.g., teaching English) and culture (e.g.,
art exhibits, readings, and ethnic crafts), but soon moved on to
doing political work such as municipal reforms (e.g., garbage
pickup and public bathhouses). The settlement house expanded
their concern for their homes and families, and extended it
into the public sphere by taking on state and federal levels on
child labor laws, factory conditions and regulation of hours
for women workers, tenement housing, and women's suffrage.
Julia Lathrop, who lived at Hull House in Chicago—the most
famous settlement house—used the thinking associated with
"activist mothering" to put forward plans to reduce poverty
by providing support for infants, children, youth, and young
adults, rather than focusing on adult poverty. In this sense, all
of America's children were Lathrop's children.[4]

The second source of the women-centered model of organizing for community change comes from African American
women. Historically, Black mothers and grandmothers were
responsible for the creation of homeplace—whether that space
be a slave hut or a wooden shack under segregation—which provided family members, and particularly the children, a space to
feel dignity, love, and respect, and a space to nurture their spirits.

Thus, homeplace was a site of resistance to white supremacy and contained a radical political element.[5] As bell hooks states:

> Despite the brutal reality of racial apartheid, of domination, one's homeplace was the one site where one could freely confront the issue of humanization, where one could resist. Black women resisted by making homes where all black people could strive to be subject, not objects, where we could be affirmed in our minds and hearts despite poverty, hardship, and deprivation, where we could restore to ourselves the dignity denied us on the outside in the public world.[6]

In addition, African American women in the 19th and 20th centuries continued this tradition of creating a space of humanization in Black women's clubs, which created orphanages, day care centers, and nursing homes. For example, Ida B. Wells was deeply involved in the women's club, and she started the first Black kindergarten in her Chicago neighborhood, helped found the National Association of Colored Women, and worked tirelessly against lynching and for the right of women to vote. Additionally, Joanne Robinson in the mid-1950s was the president of the Women's Political Council and was one of the early leaders of the Montgomery bus boycott, where she and other women mimeographed 60,000 fliers overnight and handed them out the next morning asking people not to ride the buses because of the arrest of Rosa Parks.

In the 1960s, Ella Baker created a space of humanization for young student activists as a key staff member to Dr. Martin Luther King's Southern Christian Leadership Conference (SCLC). As a leading mentor of the Student Non-Violent Coordinating Committee (SNCC), Baker promoted many of the components of a women-centered model of organizing, including group-centered leadership, facilitation, consensus decision-making, and a strong belief that the marginalized must be directly involved in the planning of the direct actions. Thus, Baker encouraged SNCC not to adopt the SCLC top-down, male, minister-dominated organizing model that tended to have a single charismatic leader. Baker was not against leadership, but rather she was against top-down, hierarchical leadership that led to the disempowerment of people. More recently, the Black Lives Matter (BLM) movement has used this group-centered model of leadership to protest police killings of African Americans. Some in the media have called BLM a leaderless movement, while Patrisse Cullors, the women who turned Black Lives Matter into a hashtag, has called it a "leader-full" movement.[7]

Saul Alinsky's Model

The second major model of local community change is Saul Alinsky's model. Saul Alinsky developed his model in Chicago in the 1940s, and he traveled throughout the nation educating marginalized communities on how to use it up until his death in 1972. The Alinsky model is based in an aggressive and confrontational stance in the public sphere where community members build an organization in order to achieve their needs through direct action. This model assumes that humans are primarily self-interested, so the most effective way to get people involved in a campaign is to appeal to their self-interest since it answers the question, "What is in it for them?" For Alinsky, power is a zero-sum game, but at the same time, he believes that the system is open to all. Therefore, the marginalized must engage as equals with the political and economic elite, and they must take power away from these groups by putting pressure on these elites through public demonstrations and activities that cannot be easily ignored. For Alinsky the goal is to win victories by being in conflict with a target. The Alinsky model uses confrontational rhetoric, which leads to military-like wins. The campaign is a battle, with organizations engaging in small-scale conflict against the people that hold power in the community, whether it be a businessman, realtor, or mayor. Importantly, Alinsky thought that the political and economic system did not need to be changed, but rather the marginalized needed to develop power so they could operate in the political sphere to get their fair share. Alinsky is not concerned about ideology, but rather about building power and winning demands that improve the lives of the have-nots.[8]

Alinsky's model has a masculine view of the public sphere, as it is seen to be competitive and conflictual. People either have power and advantage, or they are powerless and disadvantaged. To gain power, the marginalized must pick a target and, in the words of Alinsky, "freeze it, personalize it, and polarize it." Alinsky believed that the marginalized can achieve their demands by focusing on an individual rather than an institution, and this is achieved by isolating the target from other people in power and by emphasizing that the target is the problem. In addition to winning demands, the overall goal of Alinsky's model is to create an enduring organization that can compete for power in the public sphere. As people are always leaving the group, the development of new issues and constant outreach are key to an enduring organization. This male-centered model of organizing has formal spokespeople and leaders that speak for the group.[9]

In Alinsky's model, there is a divide between the person doing the organizing and the community. The organizer is someone not from the community, but rather someone who comes into the community to help build power. The expectation is that the community organizer will dedicate 24/7 to building power, and all other commitments, including family, are secondary. In order to stress that community organizing comes first, Alinsky would hold discussions and meetings late into the night for his trainees. While women were not actively discouraged from becoming community organizers, the very design of the model made it difficult for women to become a part of it, since many were expected to take care of their families. In addition, the Alinsky model draws from existing organizations (e.g., from unions, churches, ethnic clubs, bowling leagues, etc.), and the leaders come from within these organizations.[10]

Alinsky first applied his model in the slums of Chicago in 1939, when he worked to organize Poles, Slovaks, and Lithuanians into the Back of the Yards Neighborhood Council, which had the ability to turn out thousands of people to a public demonstration. Alinsky's strategy of using existing organizations and to focus direct actions on a target led to many victories, including expanded city services, free student lunch programs, and banks providing funds for mortgages and building upgrades. In 1940, Alinsky helped to create the Industrial Areas Foundation (IAF), which focused on developing community organizers using this model and helped to create IAF organizing projects throughout the nation, including SECO in Baltimore, MACO in Detroit, ACORN in Little Rock, COPS in San Antonio, and FIGHT in Rochester. While Alinsky's model of organizing has been used historically by poor communities for progressive causes, more recently the model has been used by the conservative Tea Party movement, with Dick Armey, the former Republican Congress member and House Majority Leader, promoting Alinsky's book *Rules for Radicals* as a way for the Tea Party to gain power.[11]

Alinsky's work has affected generations of community organizers, as well as the development of many important organizations and campaigns. Over the years, people have taken parts of Alinsky's model and adapted them. For example,

Alinsky's model was adapted by Fred Ross, who was the IAF West Coast Director in the late 1940s. In 1947, Ross helped to create the Community Service Organization (CSO), which moved away from finding leaders in existing organizations. The CSO recruited their leaders and participants through house meetings, and Ross developed an individual-membership model with the goal of organizing Mexican Americans to become full participants in American democracy. In Los Angeles, Ross and the CSO worked to register Latinos to vote in 1948, which led directly to the first Latino city council member in 1949. In 1950, Ross met Cesar Chavez, and Chavez immediately became involved in the CSO. Ross taught Chavez how to organize, with Chavez going on to start the United Farm Workers (UFW) along with Dolores Huerta, another Ross-trained organizer. The UFW successfully utilized Ross' individual-membership model and the house meeting to recruit new members, and the UFW used such direct actions—such as strikes, boycotts, and marches—to win union recognition, increase pay, and safer working conditions.[12]

Another organization that was started by Alinsky-trained organizers is the Association of Community Organizations for Reform Now (ACORN). In1970, George Wiley, the leader of the National Welfare Rights Organization, sent Wade Rathke to Little Rock, Arkansas, to organize the poor and welfare recipients. ACORN organized these once powerless people into a force that won a new city park, installed a new stop-light at a dangerous intersection that children often used, and stopped the practice of blockbusting, where building developers and real estate agents used fear to convince white homeowners to sell their properties at low prices, telling them Blacks would be moving in soon, and then the agent would resell the houses at much higher prices. ACORN soon expanded to six regional offices in Arkansas, and in the late 20th century expanded to

26 states with over 1,200 neighborhood chapters and 400,000 member families, with a particular focus on African American and low- to moderate-income people who worked on voter registration, predatory lending, the minimum wage, and public school funding. In 2010, conservative activists brought down ACORN by secretly videotaping two ACORN workers who appeared to provide advice on how to evade paying taxes and to set up a prostitution ring. Even though these conservative activists had tried to get numerous other ACORN employees to agree to similar things with no success, the videotape of this one case went viral, and it led to the defunding of ACORN by the federal government. With tens of millions of dollars of federal Housing and Urban Development grants no longer available, ACORN closed its doors in 2010 and filed for bankruptcy.[13]

Alinsky also influenced the development of PICO, one of the largest networks of community organizations today. The founder of PICO was John Baumann, a priest in training, who was asked by the Jesuits to go into the field. As part of his field work, Baumann attended a training by Saul Alinsky and then was given a placement with Tom Gaudette, an Alinsky lieutenant. When Baumann returned to California in 1972, he decided to start the Oakland Training Institute, a community-organizing group dedicated to improving the lives of marginalized communities in Oakland. This model was expanded to Santa Ana and San Diego, and soon after, they renamed themselves the Pacific Institute for Community Organization, or PICO. Father Baumann ran PICO as an issue-based organization for 12 years, but then moved to a faith-based model of community organizing focusing on values rather than just issues. In PICO's model, congregations from all denominations and faiths became part of the institutional base for the community organizing to occur. The glue that holds the organization together is not issues, but rather the shared values and relationships. Today, PICO stands for People Improving Communities through Organizing, and it is a national network of progressive faith-based community organizations in 150 cities and 20 states. The network provides the opportunity of PICO affiliates to work together on state or national issues, but PICO's focus is on solving the issue first at the local level.[14]

While the above organizers have adapted Alinsky's model to the current situation, others have created new models based on a sharp disagreement with the model. Feminist organizers disagree with Alinsky's unrelenting focus on conflict and competition, the belief that power is a zero-sum game, the 24/7 life of organizers, and limited leadership opportunities for the community. In addition, others disagree with Alinsky's model since it doesn't focus on issues stemming from racism, it uses mainly white staff and white institutional leaders (e.g., union officials and clergy), it requires leaders and organizers to be separate, and it fails to offer a critique of capitalism. In response, Gary Delgado, a former ACORN organizer, and Hulbert James, a former SNCC organizer, founded in 1980 the Center for Third World Organizing (CTWO) based on the belief that people of color are a colonized people in the United States and that, because of this occupied position, Asian, Black, Latino, and Native Americans should work together on anti-racist issues and diminish the lines that separate them. In the past 40 years, CTWO has trained thousands of organizers, with a particular focus on organizing urban youth.[15]

In conclusion, this section on community change is not meant to be exhaustive, but rather to highlight two of the major models of organizing and their impact on community change today. If interested in learning more, you will want to explore the rich tradition of community organizing in the labor movement and the social movement literature.

Assignment

Answer the following questions about the two models of organizing community change, integrating the text throughout your answer:

3.4 Which model of organizing for community change did you find the most and least appealing, and why?

3.5 What did you learn from the women-centered and Alinsky models of community organizing that you can directly apply to your campaign? Please integrate the text throughout your answer.

Critical Education Theory and Service-Learning

In this chapter, we have explored materialist and ideationalist categories that explain macro social change, and the women-centered and Saul Alinsky models of organizing for community change. It is time to explore how social theory explains education in general, and service-learning in particular. This exploration is important since it will help you to understand how the educational process has influenced you, and it will provide a way for you to liberate yourself from the limitations of the U.S. education system as it is currently practiced.

Two of the major social theories that examine education are functionalism and conflict theory, and each provide markedly different answers to the role of the curriculum (i.e., what is taught), the role of pedagogy (i.e., how it is taught), and the ultimate goal of education. Not surprisingly, ideationalist and materialist categories have influenced the development of functionalism and conflict theory. Functionalism, which was developed by Talcott Parson, who was influenced by Max Weber's ideationalist perspective, argues that schools provide equal education to all and that students that achieve better grades and higher test scores are more deserving since they have more talent and work harder. As a result, the schools serve as a sorting process, legitimizing the process of providing access to positions of power and status. Functionalism asserts that the function of college is as a gate-keeper, allowing the most qualified to pass through the gates while holding back the unqualified. Furthermore, higher education serves the function of selecting young adults for their future work and roles in an increasingly differentiated society. Once on a college campus, functionalists believe that students should be socialized to a set of attitudes, values, and norms that will allow alumnae to fit comfortably within the middle or upper middle class. Clearly, functionalism coincides with the current U.S. ideology of meritocracy.

On the other hand, conflict theory, which was deeply influenced by Karl Marx's materialist perspective, focuses on how the 1% uses its wealth and power to maintain and control their dominant position, which perpetuates racial, social class, and gender inequality. Conflict theorists look to the needs of the labor market to determine the manner in which school is organized. Critical to this economic model of reproduction is the concept of correspondence, which describes how the social and political institutions within a system mirror the economic institution. In education, upper-class students learn to take on leadership roles, to work independently, to be active, and to develop a value system that focuses on internalized standards of control, whereas working-class students learn through an explicit and hidden curriculum to delay gratification, be passive, and accept authority. Thus, conflict theory argues that depending on the social class of the neighborhood school, students are socialized to adopt different attitudes, values, class identifications, and self-image for their future jobs.

Critical education theory developed out of conflict theory's focus on how the 1% uses its wealth and power to maintain and control their dominant position. However, critical education theory breaks away from conflict theory's sometimes overemphasis on domination, and focuses on human agency, resistance, transformation, and the healing and repair of the world. Critical education theory is interested in developing pedagogy and curriculum that allow for schools to be agencies of change. In addition, critical education theory argues that students should actively question how power and inequality operate in society and in the classroom. Thus, critical education theory is interested in the curriculum and pedagogy that allow teachers to become "transformative intellectuals" and students to become active, critical, and engaged learners.

Critical education theory draws inspiration from Paolo Freire and Antonio Gramsci. Freire saw education as a process of liberation, and he thought that if people were put in liberating situations and were given the opportunity to solve their own problems, they could challenge oppression and create their own salvation. Freire saw the school as a site of resistance where power relations could be transformed, and not just reproduced. Gramsci, like Freire, saw people as active learners with the ability to produce knowledge and to resist relationships that are oppressive, whether they be teacher–student relationships, or ruler–ruled and leader–follower relationships. Gramsci saw the student–teacher relationship as active and reciprocal, where "every teacher is always a pupil and every pupil a teacher."[16]

Service-learning can be grounded in critical education theory because it shares the assumptions about schools being agencies of change, where students have human agency and are involved in challenging unjust social structures. Over the past 20 years, research conducted on service-learning delivered on its promises, as service-learning students—in comparison to students in a normal college course—have become more active, critical, and engaged learners as a result of interacting with various groups of people and then reflecting critically upon the meaning of those interactions.

Furthermore, policy service-learning—which focuses on changing some policy as part of their academic course work, rather than just solely integrating civic action with academic concepts—takes it to another level, since students are provided with even more opportunity for transformation, both individually and collectively, as students are able to exert their human agency by choosing what projects to work on, are given freedom to choose what strategies and actions to conduct, and have the possibility of changing an actual policy within an institution.[17]

Assignment

Integrating the text and your campaign is fundamental to "policy service-learning". With this in mind, please answer the following questions:

3.6 According to functionalism and conflict theory, what is the role of education? Do you agree with the functionalist perspective that education should legitimize the process of providing access to positions of power and status to certain qualified people, or do you agree with critical education theory that the goal of education should be for schools to be agencies of change, where students have human agency and are involved in challenging unjust social structures?

3.7 How is critical education theory similar to, but different from, conflict theory? What are the assumptions that are shared by both critical education theory and service-learning? How is critical education theory, enacted through policy service-learning, a way out of the cave and toward the light?

3.8 Is your collegiate educational experience (so far) best explained by functionalism or critical education theory?

3.9   How has this policy service-learning experience been for you so far? How is it similar to, or different from, your other college experiences?

Notes

1   Karl Marx, *The Poverty of Philosophy* (Chicago: C.H. Kerr & Company, 1920), 119.
2   Max Weber, "The Spirit of Capitalism," in Anthony Giddens and Phillip W. Sutton, eds., *Sociology: Introductory Readings* (Malden, MA: Polity Press, 2010), 110.
3   Susan Stall and Randy Stoecker, "Community Organizing or Organizing Community? Gender and the Crafts of Empowerment," *Gender and Society*, Vol. 12, No. 6, Part 1 (Dec., 1998), 729–756.
4   Julia C. Lathrop, "Child Welfare Standards: A Test of Democracy," in *Proceedings of the National Conference of Social Work at the Forty-Sixth Annual Session Held in Atlantic City, New Jersey, June 1–8, 1919* (Chicago, IL: University of Chicago Press, 1920), 5–9; Stall and Stoecker, "Community Organizing or Organizing Community?".
5   Stall and Stoecker, "Community Organizing or Organizing Community?".
6   bell hooks, *Yearning: Race, Gender, and Cultural Politics* (Boston, MA: South End Press, 1990), 42.
7   Biography.com Editors, "Ida B. Wells Biography," www.biography.com/people/ida-b-wells-9527635#later-career (accessed March 1, 2017); The Gala Group, "Black History Biographies: Ida B. Wells-Barnett," *Christian Broadcasting Network*, www.cbn.com/special/blackhistory/bio_idabwells.aspx (accessed March 1, 2017); Biography.com Editors, "Jo Ann Robinson Biography," www.biography.com/people/jo-ann-robinson-21443551#segregation-on-montgomery-buses (accessed March 1, 2017); Jocelyn McCalla, "Ella Baker: A Political Organizer's Organizer," *JMC Strategies*, http://jmcstrategies.com/2009/01/21/ella-baker-a-political-organizers-organizer (accessed March 1, 2017); Carol Mueller, "Ella Baker and the Origins of 'Participatory Democracy'," in Jacqueline Bobo, Cynthia Hudley, and Claudine Michel, eds., *Black Studies Reader* (New York, NY: Routledge, 2004), 79–90; Fredrick C. Harris, "The Next Civil Rights Movement," *Dissent*, Summer, 2015, www.dissentmagazine.org/article/black-lives-matter-new-civil-rights-movement-fredrick-harris (accessed March 3, 2017); Michele Martin, "The #BlackLivesMatter Movement: Marches and Tweets for Healing," *National Public Radio*, June 9, 2015, www.npr.org/2015/06/09/412862459/the-blacklivesmatter-movement-marches-and-tweets-for-healing (accessed March 3, 2017).
8   Saul Alinsky, *Rules for Radicals: A Practical Primer for Realistic Radicals* (New York, NY: Vintage Press, 1971); Sen, *Stir It Up*; Stall and Stoecker, "Community Organizing or Organizing Community?".

9 Alinsky, *Rules for Radicals*, 131; Stall and Stoecker, "Community Organizing or Organizing Community?".

10 Alinsky, *Rules for Radicals*; Stall and Stoecker, "Community Organizing or Organizing Community?".

11 Wendy Plotkin, "Alinsky & Back of the Yards Neighborhood Council," *COMM-ORG: The Community Organizing Website*, http://comm-org.wisc. edu/papers96/alinsky/bync.html (accessed March 4, 2017); Minieri and Gestos, *Tools for Radical Democracy*; Kenneth Vogel, "Right Loves to Hate, Imitate Alinsky," *Politico*, March 22, 2010, www.politico.com/story/2010/03/ right-loves-to-hate-imitate-alinsky-034751 (accessed March 6, 2017).

12 Sen, *Stir It Up*.

13 Richard S. Drake, "Association of Community Organizations for Reform Now," *Encyclopedia of Arkansas History & Culture*, www.encyclopediaofar-kansas.net/encyclopedia/entry-detail.aspx?entryID=4797 (accessed March 1, 2017); "ACORN Plans to Shut Down," *CNN Politics*, March 22, 2010, www. cnn.com/2010/POLITICS/03/22/us.acorn.closing (accessed March 2, 2017), "Early Growth," *Association of Community Organizations for Reform Now*, www.acorn.org/article-list/early-growth.html (accessed March 2, 2017).

14 "The Pico Organizing Model," *PICO National Network*, www.piconetwork. org/about/model (accessed March 2, 2017); "Father John Baumann, SJ, Discusses PICO and Community Organizing for Passionate Leaders in Social Entrepreneurship Speaker Series," *Holy Names University*, October 31, 2014, www.hnu.edu/about/news/father-john-baumann-sj-discusses-pico-and-community-organizing-passionate-leaders-social (accessed March 2, 2017).

15 Sen, *Stir It Up*; "CTWO's History," *Center for Third World History*, http:// ctwo.org/home-page/about/history (accessed March 3, 2017).

16 Antonio Gramsci, *Selections from Prison Notebooks*, in Quintin Hoare and Geoffrey Smith, eds. (New York, NY: International, 1971), 349–50.

17 Peter McLaren and Rhonda Hammer, "Critical Pedagogy and the Postmodern Challenge: Towards a Critical Postmodernist Pedagogy of Liberation," *Journal of Educational Foundations*, Vol. 3, No. 3 (1989), 29; Henry Giroux, *Teachers as Intellectuals: Toward a Critical Pedagogy of Learning* (Westport, CT: Bergin & Garvey, 1988).

4

BUILDING POWER

Now that your group has had the chance to reflect on various theories and models of social change, it is time to turn our attention to building the power necessary to win your campaign. First, we will discuss what is power and how to get it, and then we will explore how to recruit people to build your base.

Some of you might be squeamish when it comes to power. You might find power repugnant since power has been used throughout history to dominate people. However, power doesn't have to be oppressive. Dr. Martin King thought that one of the greatest problems in history was that power and love were often seen as polar opposites rather than as complementary to each other. King stated, "[P]ower without love is reckless and abusive, and love without power is sentimental and anemic. Power at its best is love implementing the demands of justice, and justice at its best is power correcting everything that stands against love." In addition, you might not relate to power because you don't see yourself as powerful. This quote—often attributed to President Nelson Mandela, but really the words of the author Marianne Williamson—gets at the possibility of not wanting to step into our power:

> Our deepest fear is not that we are inadequate. Our deepest fear is that we are powerful beyond measure. It is our light,

not our darkness, that most frightens us. We ask ourselves,
Who am I to be brilliant, gorgeous, talented, fabulous?

Clearly, this book is calling you to become individually empowered and for your group to become powerful. Generally, social
change groups don't start out powerful, but go through a process
of developing power. This chapter is dedicated to the purpose of
your group gaining power.[1]

What Is Power

Power is the ability to accomplish what you want done. In the
world of organizing, power provides the strength to bring about
political, social, and economic change. As Walter Reuther, the
president of United Auto Workers (UAW), stated, "Power is the
ability of a labor union like UAW to make the most powerful
corporation in the world, General Motors, say yes when it wants
to say no." Thus, your group needs to figure out a way to get
power so you can accomplish what you want done. The question
is, what type of power?[2]

There are three types of power: power over, power with, and
power for. *Power over* is where an individual, organization, or
the state uses its power to limit or expand rights or resources.
Historically, power over has been used by the few to dominant
and oppress the larger population. However, in social action,
power over can be conceptualized to mean that a community
organization develops its power so that it can match, or even
overcome, the power of the economic and political elites so as to
win the demand. This assertion of power that matches or over-
comes the power of the economic and political elite is seen as a
positive and is in alignment with Alinsky's model of organizing
for community change.[3]

Power with is when people share power with each other. Generally, power with stems from collective non-violent activity,

where group members work together in an organization where power is shared, and decisions are made collectively. At the organizational level, power with focuses on facilitation, consensus decision-making, and group-centered leadership. This vision of power with is in alignment with the women-centered model of community organizing.[4]

Power for is when an individual or an organization advocates on behalf of a person. Community organizers generally do not like this type of power, since it disempowers the group that is most affected. However, it is possible that a group cannot make the demands themselves (e.g., a group that is so weakened by an event, perhaps after a natural disaster) and so power for might be utilized by advocates.

In addition, power manifests itself in three forms: organized people, organized money, and organized violence. *Organized people*, which is the focus of this book, is where community members who are many times marginalized come together to work collectively on the enactment of a demand that they have to improve their community (at least, from their perspective). In addition to working on campaigns, organized people can also work through political parties, non-violent social movements, and within institutions.[5]

Organized money is where people from the economic elite (i.e., the 1% and above) come together and use their collective wealth and influence to work for policies that are beneficial to their interests. This takes the form of creating think tanks and political action committees (PACs), hiring lobbyists, and making donations to politicians, all with the goal of promoting policies and legislation to benefit the economic elite. Not surprisingly, organized people are often fighting against organized money. And while it is not a fair fight when it comes to resources, I have found that it is possible for organized people to triumph.[6]

The third way power manifests itself is *organized violence*. Organized violence is used by the state (military and police) to maintain power and control over other states and foreign combatants, and over groups and individuals. The military and police use violence and the threat of violence to maintain control. At the same time, revolutionary groups also use organized violence in their attempt to change the status quo. Lastly, organized crime and gangs employ organized violence to control a community through the use of violence and intimidation. I reject organized violence in all its forms (with the exception of self-defense), so it will not be discussed any further.[7]

Assignment

4.1   How do you feel about power? Do you have negative or positive feelings about power? Do you shy away from power, or do you like to feel powerful?

4.2   Please provide an example of organized people within your campus community, city, county, or state. What initially brought the group together? How long have they been working together? Did they have to confront organized money or organized violence? Name some examples of organized money and organized violence.

4.3   What types of power (i.e., power over, power with, or power for) do you think your group will use in your campaign?

How to Get Power

You get power by becoming organized. Recall, this book is about *organized people*, where community members come together to work collectively on the enactment of a demand to improve their community. The first step, which you have already completed, is to get a group of people to come together to fight for a demand. In the language of community organizing, your group is the "organizing committee".

The next step is to find more people to work on the issue. The more people you have involved in your campaign means the more power it has, since if you hold a rally and ten people show up, the media and your opponents may come to the conclusion that you don't have much support. However, if you have 100 people at a rally, the media and your opponents may come to the determination that many in the community support your campaign. In addition, more people lets your group do more work, whether that is making phone calls, putting up fliers, writing letters to the editor, or getting people to come to your events. I will discuss how recruitment is key to building your base later in this chapter.

Another step to become organized is to ally with the groups that are already working on the demand or might have an interest in doing so. In Chapter 5 you will be exploring which groups you might become allies with as part of your power map, and in Chapter 6 you will decide whether you need allies, and if so, you will be reaching out to them to join the campaign. Identifying possible allies is an extremely important part of your campaign, as allies can bring with them more people and resources for the campaign. In Chapter 1, you began this process by talking to a couple of stakeholders (i.e., potential allies) about your issue. Your group will want to continue and expand on these stakeholder contacts in the coming weeks. As you move forward, partnering with allies may impact the structure of the "organizing committee", as these allies might join it, or they might remain separate, and your group might be the "student wing" of a larger coalition.

In Chapter 5 you will also conduct an historical analysis of your issue, which will help develop more power, as there is nothing more powerful than well-informed group members. As

Steve Biko, the South African activist and martyr, once stated, "The most potent weapon in the hands of the oppressor is the mind of the oppressed."[8] Thus, your group gains power by knowing the issue well and demonstrating publicly your knowledge. As the old adage goes, "knowledge is power", since the more you know, the more you will be able to control events. Furthermore, your group gains power when you and the other members develop your knowledge and skills to conduct social action, whether that be to learn the various strategies and tactics of community change (Chapter 6), to work with the media (Chapter 7), to learn how to create a well-functioning group (Chapter 8), or to write a plan to keep the campaign on track (in Chapter 9). In addition, you can develop your knowledge and skills at events sponsored by local non-profit and campus organizations that focus on leadership development.

Lastly, your group gains power if you win your demand. It is similar to winning more chips when playing a card game. However, instead of it being a card game, you get a few more chips to play in the next campaign. Your group gets these "chips" because you have been effective at getting something done, which is at the heart of the definition of power. Thus, if your group wins a campaign, you have more power for future campaigns, as allies and opponents will take your group seriously.

Recruitment: Base-Building for Power

As stated above, more people equals more power, and in social action, the main way to get more people involved in the campaign is to recruit new members. Recruitment is key to the success of campaigns since new members provide more numbers to do the work and help mobilize more people to take action. Thus, your group continually needs to be building and increasing your base of support. It is also important to build your base because your group will always be losing some folks as they leave to do other things, whether it be to focus on grades, work, or family. Thus, your group needs to recruit new members continuously throughout the campaign. To achieve this end, I recommend that one or two group members volunteer to head up a *recruitment team*. While many group members will be involved in the recruiting process, it is very important that one or two students focus on it. During the meetings, they will be the members to ensure that the group is fulfilling its recruitment plan (i.e., putting up fliers tabling, and giving classroom presentations, etc.).

As your recruitment team becomes established, here are a few things you will want to consider. First, go to places where there are a lot of people. On a college campus, these places are generally in front of the student union, library, or large academic building, or by the parking garage. If your issue focuses on a community issue, a good place to recruit is in front of the library, or town square, at a farmer's market, or community event, or some other place where people gather. You can just stand out in front of these areas with a clipboard, but it is nice if you have a small table set up with a campaign sign in front to attract attention. A key point to recruiting is that you don't want to spend too much time with each person. If they are interested, great! Get them to sign your signup sheet. If you talk too long to any one person, you may miss out on the opportunity to talk to other students walking by. If they aren't interested, that is fine too, as there are more people to talk to. Another great place to recruit on a campus is in the classroom. Many professors will let you give a 1–2-minute presentation about an activity you are involved with.[9]

Second, your group needs to develop an *organizational rap*. An organizational rap is a 1–2-minute presentation that explains your issue, and is used to entice people to join your group or to participate in an upcoming event. Of course, your organizational rap will want to frame the issue so that it expresses the values of your group and connects to the shared values of the people you are presenting to. You will use the organizational rap when you are presenting in a classroom or "tabling" in front of an academic building.[10]

After creating your organizational rap, you need to develop several recruitment tools. First, you will need to create a *signup sheet* where people interested in the campaign can write down their name and contact information. This signup sheet will be used anytime you make contact with new folks. After they sign the sheet, you will want to "work the list", which involves contacting them in the following 24–48 hours, thanking them for their interest, and inviting them personally to your next meeting or event. Realize that if you have ten to 20 names written down, the likelihood is that two or three might come to a meeting or event, and one might join your group.[11]

You also need to make a *flier* for your group. Fliers on a college campus are an important way to get the word out about your issue, and it is a great way to get name recognition for your group. The flier should be colorful and include a statement and image that is catchy and engaging. It should also have the group's name and contact information. Where you put the fliers is important. Obviously, high traffic areas are the best. Unfortunately, "flier wars" can occur with all the various campus groups vying to be heard. Try to place your flier in the best visual space. Never rip down another flier, as this is bad etiquette, but it is all right to move another group's flier over a few inches in order for your flier to be seen.

Another recruitment tool is through *social media*, so your group will want to create Facebook and Twitter accounts. On the webpage and feeds, you should include your group's name, an explanation of the issue, and contact information. However, unlike a flier, which is static, you can post updates about your group's campaign and upcoming events. If you are using Twitter, you can tap into a much larger network of groups and individuals by using hashtags that have been created by others (e.g., #fightfor15). Almost all my student groups use social media as part of their recruitment strategy, as well as to inform the larger community about upcoming events and the status of the campaign. However, it should be noted that their efforts have not generated the kind of interest generated by other activists. Clearly, social media is a powerful tool, as can be seen by how effective it was in informing people and energizing them to action during the Arab Spring and the Women's Day March on Washington, DC. However, my students have had limited success using it and have had more success in getting people to attend events by talking to people face to face or by calling them.

Assignment

Your group needs to develop a recruitment plan. In your plan, you should determine:

4.4 Where your group plans to recruit on campus (e.g., in front of buildings, classrooms, and/or dorms);

4.5 Who is going to recruit at these sites, and on what days and times throughout the term;

4.6 What classrooms you are going to visit, and who is going to do the presentation, and on what day and time;

4.7 Who is going put up your group's fliers, and in what halls and buildings will the fliers be put in;

4.8 Who will post the information to your social media accounts;

4.9 How large your group needs to be to win your campaign, and how many recruitment events you need to reach that goal. You might want to estimate how many people you can get to sign your signup sheet every time you set up a table in front of a building, or how many students you can get to sign after a classroom presentation.

4.10 Lastly, create a sign-up sheet, flier, social media accounts, and a 1–2 minute organizational rap, along with your group. Upon completion of your organizational rap, you should practice it in front of your classmates.

In responding to the above questions, the more detailed and specific you are in your answers, the better your recruitment plan will be. In addition, remember that in an academic term, you have limited time to act (i.e., three to four months); thus, the sooner you start to take action the better, so start recruiting now. Remember, your group must develop a 1–2-minute organizational rap, flier, sign-up sheet, and social media account.

The sign-up sheet should have a place to write down the name, phone number, and email of people interested in the campaign. You might also want to leave a space to make any notes, so you can indicate if they have a high, medium, or low interest in your issue.

As stated above, your flier should be colorful, and include a catchy statement, the group's name and contact information. You should follow this same advice for all your social media accounts.

For the organizational rap, your group should come up with a uniform statement, but afterwards you will want to add your own specific language to make it yours. You want the rap to feel natural and comfortable, and by adding your own words and flair, it will make it more your own, and you will be more comfortable saying it. At the same time, you want to stay on message, so don't change the basic themes and ideas. The rap should not be longer than two minutes or 120 seconds. The below guidelines highlight eight points to make, so you can to consider this your "8 in 120" group exercise. The organizational rap should include:

1. *An introduction of who you are and what your group is doing* (e.g., Hi, I am Leila from *CAFÉ J*, and we are working on raising the minimum wage from $8 to $10).

2. *A question about your issue that raises interest* (e.g., How many of you make minimum wage?). Sometimes you might want to start with a question, and then introduce who you are.

3. *A statement about your past accomplishments* (e.g., *CAFÉ J* has built a large coalition with non-profits and labor and faith groups to pass our ballot initiative in November).

4. *Information about the issue to politically educate* (e.g., Did you know that rent in San Jose is $1,600, and that if you work full-time at a minimum-wage job, you make only $1,300, not even enough to cover your rent, let alone your food, transportation, and other needs?).

5. *A proposed solution* (e.g., *CAFÉ J* proposes to increase the minimum wage by $2 in order to help over 40,000 San Jose workers, including some of you, to pay for the basics like food, clothing, and school).

6. *Ask them to do something* (e.g., Can you come to today's rally at noon in front of the Chamber of Commerce, which is the leader of the opposition to raise the minimum wage?).

7. *Ask them to attend your next meeting or an upcoming event* (e.g., *CAFÉ J* meets every Tuesday night at 7 pm in the 4th floor lounge of the MLK Library. Can you come?).

8. *Give them your contact information* (email and phone number). If you are speaking to a group, pass around a signup sheet to sign. If you are speaking to an individual, ask them to fill out your signup sheet.[12]

People Came, Now What?

Success! People have attended a meeting or an event! So what do you do now? First, thank them for coming, and then at the end of the meeting or event, thank them again. Just because they came once to a meeting or an event is no guarantee that they will come back. The reality is that students are extremely busy, and you will have a much greater chance of keeping them involved in your campaign if they feel they are appreciated, so start with gratitude. Second, people will return if they become actively engaged in the issue. Thus, find something for them to do for your group as soon as possible, no matter how small. It might be as small as asking them to set up the room at the next meeting or event. You might also call on them during the meeting so they have the opportunity to participate. The key thing is to engage them so they start developing a connection to the issue and to your group. Over time, you will want to give them more responsibility, eventually providing them the opportunity to become more deeply involved in the campaign. For example, you might want to invite a person who has come to a few meetings to work on the recruitment committee or some other committee that you have formed. The important part is to get the person to enter into a relationship with your organization and to provide them the opportunity to develop as a leader and to begin taking responsibility for the campaign. In the world of social change, this process of persuading people to take action is called mobilization.[13]

One last thing to remember: don't just recruit just at the beginning of the campaign, but throughout it. This requires that you stick to your recruitment plan, and don't forget to include recruiting from the beginning to the end of the campaign. In fact, at every event you hold, the group should actively recruit new members, as well as identify people who are part of other groups who might want to support the campaign. Often the last event you hold is the one you want the most people at, so recruit to the end of the campaign.

Case Studies

My students have been effective at recruiting people to their events. This is due to the fact that all of them must develop a good organizational rap. Here is an example of an organizational rap from *Hungry Spartans*, which was advocating for a centralized food pantry on campus.

> Hello, my name is Ariana, and I am here with *Hungry Spartans* to discuss the current food crisis we are having here at San Jose State.
>
> Do you believe that food should be the last of any students' worries at SJSU? Do you believe that all students have a right to access healthy and affordable food? As of now, one out of three students on campus face food insecurity and miss at least one meal daily. Why do you think this is? I am here to talk about a proposal for a centralized food pantry at San Jose State.
>
> We currently have 14 food pantries on campus, but they are not very accessible. Most students do not even know where they are located. Also, the university does not pay for these pantries. Students contribute about $2,000 per month so that the food pantries are stocked. This payment doesn't even meet the needs of these students.
>
> Recently we have been given the opportunity to partner up with Second Harvest Food bank for FREE donations of a variety of food options. We, the *Hungry Spartans*, demand a centralized food pantry to be placed in the Student Health Center. This location would be accessible and provide a de-stigmatized space that can be easily reached by trucks. Right now, the only thing stopping us from getting a food pantry is the problem of space. Some people in power do not want to provide us a space for a pantry, or they say that space is unavailable, and yet space is always provided for students in extracurricular activities. Do you think this is right? Do you think this is an important issue?

We need your help and support. We need your voice to let the administration know that students at SJSU are hungry. Tuition and the price of living have made it difficult for students to access food, and we demand a centralized food pantry on campus that is accessible to students. Will you sign and add your contact information to show your support? We'd love to have you on board and supporting us.

As stated above, a common activity of recruiting on campuses is "tabling", which involves standing in front of a table and giving your organizational rap to students who are walking by. As students are often in a hurry, running between classes or going to eat, it is tough to get them to stop. To get students to stop and talk, you will want to come up with an interesting opening line. *Students for Dudley Moorehead Hall* (*DMH*), a group advocating for air conditioning in all the classrooms and offices of a 1950s building, where temperatures often reached 90 degrees in the afternoons, would ask students walking into the building, "Are you hot?" This generally stopped the students and gave group members the opportunity to give their organizational rap. In addition, to cool students down, they would provide them with water, popsicles, and a hand fan with "Students for DMH" printed on it. These creative actions made the whole interaction fun for the group members and the students entering the building.

In addition, *Students for DMH* created this flier (Figure 4.1), which they plastered around the building.

Students for DMH also created a Facebook page and used it to highlight both their past and upcoming events. The Facebook page included the group's and their issue, and provided images from their "faint in" action. Interestingly, *Students for DMH* were both self-interested in their demand for air conditioning, as they wanted it cooler in the building for themselves, but they were also concerned for future students.

Figure 4.1 Students for DMH flier.

As discussed above, an effective way to recruit is to table in front of an area where there are a lot of students. Figure 4.2 is a photo of tabling by students from the *College Awareness Network* (*CAN*), a group whose demand was for the institutionalization of a program to encourage third grade students to attend campus by giving them an informative tour of the campus. In order to

Figure 4.2 Students tabling for the *College Awareness Network*. From left to right: Norma Alegria, Lindsey Forbes, Lorena Gonzalez, Tiffany Rivera, and Becca Fulcher.

get students to stop and talk to them, the *College Awareness Network* put out candy by their signup sheet. It was highly effective!

Privilege and Power: A Word of Caution

As part of the organizing committee, you are a leader. This means that you are taking responsibility for the group, thinking about its needs, and helping it function effectively by putting forward creative solutions. In this role, you may be a listener or learner, a motivator or convener, an agitator to move people to act or a critical thinker looking at all the angles, or someone who steps up to challenge a racist or sexist comment. Whatever role you take, it is important to think about your own privilege and power—or lack of it—particularly those awarded to you by your race, gender, social class, sexual orientation, immigration status, and religious affiliation. The reality is that some of these classifications have more status and privilege than others in society. This means that if you have some privilege, or if you are even over-privileged, you need to reflect upon how this will affect your social action work. At the same time, if you lack privilege in some areas, you will want to reflect upon how this will affect your social action work, as well.

This reflection is important to do, as you will be working with communities and organizing social actions. How the on- or off-campus community perceives you will depend on what privileges you have, as well as how you present yourself. If, as students, you are minimum-wage workers, and you are organizing other minimum-wage workers in the community, you will have a better chance to be seen by the community as co-workers in the struggle for justice. However, if, as students, you come from the upper class, or your group is predominantly white, and you are working with low-wage workers or people of color, you may be seen as outsiders coming into their community, and folks might be concerned about working together. In my opinion, it is better to have open discussions with your potential allies about the possible imbalance of privilege and power. Through open dialogue, it is possible to figure out ways to work together. For example, the student group *Collective Voices for Undocumented Students* had both undocumented and documented students working together. They figured out how to work together successfully by giving primacy to the voices of the undocumented students. Lucila Ortiz, a student in *Collective Voices for Undocumented Students*, explains that it was important

> that the voices of the undocumented members were the most heard. If a discussion was in a place in one of our meetings and there was a disagreement, members of the group would ask undocumented students for their opinions. Also, if the discussion was dominated by documented members, others would be very conscious and highlight the need for undocumented members to speak up.

So, while there was a clear difference of privilege in the group, the students figured out a way to overcome this imbalance and to work together.

Assignment

4.10   Explain which of the following characteristics (e.g., race, gender, social class, sexual orientation, educational attainment, immigration status, and religious affiliation) provide you with the most and least privilege and power in U.S. society.

4.11   What ways might your background (i.e., your race, gender, social class, sexual orientation, educational attainment, immigration status, and religious affiliation) help or hinder you in your social action work?

4.12   As a college student, what privileges do you have and how do they play out?

4.13   How will your group be sensitive to the possible imbalance of privilege and power within your group, as well as the possible imbalance of privilege and power with the groups you might be working with?

Notes

1 Martin Luther King, "Where Do We Go from Here," in James M. Washington, ed., *A Testament of Hope: The Essential Writings of Martin Luther King Jr.* (San Francisco: Harper and Row, 1986), 247; Marianne Williamson, *A Return to Love: Reflections on the Principles of a Course in Miracles.* (New York: HarperOne, 1996), 190.
2 King, "Where Do We Go from Here," 246.
3 Minieri and Gestos, *Tools for Radical Democracy.*
4 Minieri and Gestos, *Tools for Radical Democracy.*
5 Minieri and Gestos, *Tools for Radical Democracy.*
6 Minieri and Gestos, *Tools for Radical Democracy.*
7 Minieri and Gestos, *Tools for Radical Democracy.*
8 Steve Biko, *I Write What I Like*, University of Chicago Press Books, www.press.uchicago.edu/ucp/books/book/chicago/I/bo3632310.html (accessed March 30, 2017).
9 Minieri and Gestos, *Tools for Radical Democracy*; Sen, *Stir It Up.*
10 Minieri and Gestos, *Tools for Radical Democracy*; Sen, *Stir It Up.*
11 Minieri and Gestos, *Tools for Radical Democracy*; Sen, *Stir It Up.*
12 Minieri and Gestos, *Tools for Radical Democracy*; Sen, *Stir It Up.*
13 Minieri and Gestos, *Tools for Radical Democracy*; Colin Delaney, "Mobilization: Getting People to Act on Your Behalf," *Epolitics.com*, April 4, 2002, www.epolitics.com/2012/04/04/mobilization-getting-people-to-act-on-your-behalf (accessed April 25, 2017).

5
RESEARCH

By the third or fourth week of the campaign you have identified your issue and you have begun developing, and possibly started to implement, your recruitment plan. Now is the time to do research. Research is critical because you need to learn as much as possible about the history of your issue, about your target's position about your issue, about the other stakeholders that care about your issue, and about the level of power these potential allies or opponents have to support or defeat you. This part of the campaign is particularly relevant since this is what you are supposed to be doing in college, that is, examining, analyzing, explaining, and interpreting information. The research you are about to do will make you an expert on your issue. This will help overcome the do-gooder label, one who has their heart in the right place but doesn't really know about the real world. Also, the more you know about the issue, the more your allies and opponents will take you seriously. Remember, knowledge is power.

Historical and Target Analyses, and Power Mapping

There are three parts to your research: (1) historical analysis, (2) target analysis, and (3) power mapping. Your research starts with learning about the national and local history of the social problem, as well as attempts to solve it. As part of this historical analysis, you will want to know what solutions from the past and present have worked, and what has not worked. In addition, you will want to know what individuals and organizations have been the major players, both nationally and locally, working on the social problem, and what has been their frameworks to explain the social program and solution. Lastly, you will want to explore how social class, race, and gender have affected the history of your issue, and what were the ideological arguments surrounding the issue. Generally, social problems and solutions have long histories. For example, poverty in the United States has been a major problem since the founding of country, and there have been numerous attempts to solve it, from Thomas Paine's idea for social insurance for the elderly in 1797, to Jacob Coxey's idea for public works in 1894, to the more recent War on Poverty in 1964. In addition to learning the national and local history, you need to learn who have been the major stakeholders when it comes to your issue, and how they have framed the problem and solutions. Sometimes your historical analysis will lead you to explore U.S. capitalism itself. If this is the case, I tell my students that this is a positive, as I believe every democratic citizen living in the United States needs to do a close analysis of both the positives and negatives of American capitalism. After writing up the historical analysis, I recommend that one or two group members volunteer to head up a *research team* in order to follow your issue, and the organizations and individuals involved, in the press and social media.[1]

Second, your group needs to learn as much as you can about your target, which is the lowest ranking person that can meet your demand. Most importantly, you need to find out your target's position on your issue. In addition, you need to learn what is the political lens that your target sees the world from, what are the target's interests, what other things does your target care about, whom does the target listen to, how much power does the target possess, under what conditions does the target give in, and how does the target counterattack. If the lowest ranking decision-maker is not a person, but rather a committee or council, you will still want to personalize them. The goal then becomes targeting the individual members of the committee or council in order to win a majority of the voting body. Your campaign will also want to determine if there is a secondary target in your campaign, which is someone who can pressure or persuade the primary target. If you do find a secondary target, you can target them as well, in the hope that they can persuade the primary target to agree to your demands.[2]

By conducting a target analysis, your group will be able to focus your campaign message so that it is effective, since the goal is to move the target and get them to agree to your demand. The goal of the target analysis is to find information that will help you get your target to agree with your demands, especially if they are lukewarm or opposed to them. It will also help you when you meet the target and ask them to say "yes" to your demand. Negotiating with the target is a key part of any campaign and will be discussed in more detail in Chapter 9. After writing up the target analysis, I recommend that a group member volunteers to join the research team in order to follow the target's actions and statements in the press and social media. If your group is small, you may want to have one of the people who already joined the research team now take on following the target in the media. If your group is mid-size to large, you can have another person join the research team, as this provides an opportunity for more group members to become intimately connected to the campaign.[3]

Third, your group needs to do a power map of your issue, which involves mapping out who has the power in the community. Recall that power is the ability to achieve purpose, and you need to figure out how much power your group possesses and how much power you will need to win the campaign. This assessment of your organizational power and capacity to move the target is extremely important so as to understand your chances of winning the campaign. It will also help your group determine if you need to get more power by recruiting new members, creating more actions to publicly demonstrate your power, or building alliances with other organizations. Thus, your power map will want to include an analysis of the power of your potential allies. After finishing the power map, if you decide that your group alone cannot generate enough power to win the campaign and that it needs more power to do so, you will want to take the information generated by this power map and use it in Chapter 6 to contact these potential allies to see if they want to join the campaign. Power mapping also includes an assessment of the power of your potential opponents who have the capacity to defeat your group. This part of the power map is essential since your group needs to know how powerful your opposition is and attempt to determine if it is possible to defeat them.

Ultimately, whether or not you win your campaign will depend on how much power your side has and how well it exerts its powers. It will also depend on how much power your opposition has, and whether it decides to exert its power or decides to sit on the sidelines. If your opposition decides to sit on the sidelines, it will be much easier to win. There are many reasons why your opposition might not exert its power. It might be due to the fact that they have other priorities, or it could be due to the fact that your group has struck a deal with your opposition, agreeing to one of your demands rather than all three.

Case Studies

Case Study: Historical Analysis

The *Campus Alliance for Economic Justice* (*CAFÉ J*) began humbly, as most campaigns do. On the second day of class, Marisela put forward her idea of increasing the minimum wage in Santa Clara County, and she recruited three students to work on this campaign. In the second week of the semester, the students began to do their historical research, and within a few days, they learned that it was not possible to raise the minimum wage in the county, which was composed of 15 cities, because the legal authority to enforce a minimum wage came from the individual cities. Thus, the historical research conducted by the students provided invaluable information, as it forced the students early on to choose which city in the county to try and raise the minimum wage in. San Jose was the largest city in the county (almost one million people), and the university was based in San Jose, so it was an easy decision. The students would focus on San Jose.

Over the next week, the historical research produced more information to guide their campaign. In that first month, the students learned that over the past 30 years, three cities—San Francisco, Santa Fe, and Washington, DC—had increased the minimum wage. Additionally, the students found research that showed that the impact of these city-wide minimum-wage increases: (1) helped low-wage workers pay for basic needs like food and rent; (2) stimulated the local economy, since the people making the minimum wage spent these few extra dollars locally; (3) did not increase unemployment; and (4) did not hurt small business, because they generally passed on this cost by raising prices by a small percentage. This information was critical since it allowed the students to be confident that what they were proposing would not hurt small businesses nor increase unemployment, two concerns that stakeholders had raised. It also allowed the students to speak confidently to the media about their campaign. When the students cited this research to the press, which had been conducted by leading economists in the field, it was possible to make a convincing case for raising the minimum wage. This research also provided the students the necessary information they needed to combat the Chamber of Commerce and Restaurant Association, two powerful groups they had learned about in their historical analysis, and who would go on to actively and vigorously oppose the minimum-wage campaign.

Once *CAFÉ J* completed their historical analysis, and they were talking to the community about their solution, they were told by the local labor advocates that in order for them to be involved, *CAFÉ J* would need to conduct a scientific poll and that the poll needed to show strong support for raising the minimum wage. This led *CAFÉ J*, in conjunction with the university's Survey and Policy Research Institute, to conduct a scientific poll to determine the level of support among city voters. The poll cost $6,000, which is about one-sixth the normal price. The reason the poll was so inexpensive was that the students provided the majority of the labor to make the phone calls. The results of the poll were very positive, as it showed that 70% of the voters supported a $2 increase in the minimum wage. Once again, research gave students the information they needed to convince others to support the campaign. It also allowed students to feel confident that they had created a policy that the vast majority of citizens supported. Lastly, the poll gave *students in CAFE J* the opportunity to become deeply involved in the campaign.

Another example of an historical analysis impacting a campaign can be found with *Students for Campus Safety*. As part of this group's historical analysis, the students researched how many campus emergency phone towers had been built on campus. These emergency phone towers had a built-in intercom system, which would connect the caller directly to the university police department, as well as a blue light on top of the metal poll. When activated, the blue light would flash, and the intercom system would connect the caller to the campus police, with the goal of getting an officer to the site immediately. To find out the exact number of campus emergency phone towers, the students walked around the university and then created a campus map of the "blue lights". This information helped *Students for Campus Safety* to win their demand. When this student group met with the campus police chief, the students presented them with the map of the campus emergency phone towers; incredibly, the police chief conceded that he didn't even have such a map of the phone towers. Thus, the students provided the police chief with the information that he needed in order to make a decision about the students' demand to increase the number of campus emergency phone towers on campus. It also put the students in a powerful position since they had more information about the issue than even their target, the police chief. Knowledge is power.

The historical research that *Students for DMH* conducted was also crucial to winning their campaign. As part of the group's historical research, *Students for DMH* found out that Dudley Moorehead Hall was constructed in the 1950s. The students also learned that at schools with a large population of working-class students of color, the students were twice as likely to be in buildings that were built in the 1950s and that many of them were without air conditioning. This information provided them with the frame that they were being treated unfairly due to their social class and race and ethnicity. Furthermore, the students had discovered through their research that over the past 20 years, Dudley Moorehead Hall was scheduled to be knocked down and replaced multiple times. However, there was never enough money in the campus budget to do so. Thus, when the students presented their demands, and the university stated that air conditioning in Dudley Moorehead Hall would be a waste of money since they were going to knock the building down in the near future, the students pointed to the fact that the administration had been claiming they were going to knock it down for over 20 years, and that this position was actually an excuse for inaction. Additionally, *Students for DMH* did a cost estimate to air condition the entire building, which provided the president and provost with specific numbers to say yes or no to. All of these actions by *Students for DMH* were made possible as a result of the students' research.

Case Study: Target Analysis

Sometimes the lowest ranking person who can meet your demand is an administrator within an organization. For the *College Awareness Network*, which was working to institutionalize a campus tour program for third graders, the lowest ranking person was a staff person in the Office of Student Affairs. In addition, for *Every 15 Minutes a Student Waits*, whose demand was to increase the number of printers in the Dr. Martin Luther King Jr. Library, which was open to the public as well as the students, the lowest ranking person was the dean of the library. However, sometimes the lowest ranking person that can meet your demand is the head of an organization; for *Students Against Sweatshops*, whose demand was to join the Worker's Rights Consortium, the lowest ranking person was the university president.

CAFÉ J's campaign to raise the minimum wage had a unique target, which was the voting population. In this campaign, the students learned from a second poll that was conducted that liberals and the middle and working classes would strongly support an increase to the minimum wage. At the same time, the increase in the minimum wage had little support with white, conservative males making over $100,000. Since the campaign had such few resources, limited energy was spent with these above groups, as they were going to support it or oppose it regardless of what they heard. However, the poll showed that conservative women and the Vietnamese population had not yet made their decision about minimum wage, so the campaign's limited resources went to encourage these two groups to support it. Both of these groups ended up providing more than 50% support to the minimum-wage increase, so the information that was gathered through our target research, once again, proved decisive. Interestingly, while the campaign targeted the voters in the city, as it was a ballot measure, *CAFÉ J* and their allies also tried to convince the San Jose City Council to just pass the legislation themselves. Five months before the election, the city council met and voted on whether to put it on the ballot, or to just pass it right on the spot. This choice is given to the city council as part of California's election law. Thus, during this period of time, the targets became four city council members, and the students and their allies tried to get them to enact it without going to the ballot. However, this effort was not successful, and it went to the ballot, and was passed by 60% of the voters. *San Joseans for a World-Class City*, a student group dedicated to increasing the local business tax on mid-size to large corporations, also targeted voters and city council members, as they too worked on a ballot measure.

Lastly, students working on the *Gulf Coast Civic Works Project*, which worked to create 100,000 living-wage jobs for Gulf Coast residents to rebuild their communities, targeted Senator Barack Obama during the 2008 presidential race. The target information gathered on Senator Obama became helpful when he was elected president and was used by the campaign to construct a letter asking him to sign an executive order creating a Gulf Coast public works project. The historical research also connected the campaign to the activists who had showed Senator Obama around New Orleans, and it was these community leaders who signed the campaign's letter to President-Elect Obama to sign an executive order. In addition, Congresswoman Nancy Pelosi, the Speaker of the House, was a target of the *Gulf Coast Civic Works Project*, as the students tried to get her to agree to hold a congressional hearing for their bill. As part of their target analysis, the students found that she was a devout Catholic, so the students made an unsuccessful attempt to ask a secondary target, the bishop of San Francisco, to persuade Speaker Pelosi to hold a public hearing on the Gulf Cast Civic Works Act.

Case Study: Power Mapping

Student groups have used the construction of their power map to help them win several campaigns. As a result of their power map, *Students Against Sweatshops* realized the campus president was politically weak. The faculty was considering a strike for higher pay, and the president had been receiving negative press about the university's stand against the strike. Also, students had led a series of anti-war protests on campus, and *Students Against Sweatshops* came to the conclusion that the president might be more willing to accede to their demand because he felt under siege. The last thing the president would want is to have another group publicly demanding something from him. The students' analysis proved to be correct, for shortly after the group met with the president, the students were told that they had won their demand as the president had agreed to sign on to the Worker's Rights Consortium.

CAFÉ J students did a power map of San Jose, and they came to the conclusion that they could get the labor, non-profit, and faith communities to support an increase in the minimum wage. Furthermore, they determined that this collective strength would provide the campaign with enough power to win their demand. The students' power map showed that the Chamber of Commerce, which they predicted would be the main group to oppose the campaign, would not have enough power to stop a unified community. Once again, the students were correct. As part of their power map, *CAFÉ J* students identified the relative power of each of the ten city council members and the mayor.

Incredibly, by the end of the campaign, the students knew all the names of the city council members and mayor, and had talked to several of them personally. This led the students to feel like "power players" in the community, and enhanced their belief in civic engagement and increased their own sense of power. When the mayor called the increase to San Jose's minimum wage the greatest threat to the downtown in his "state of the city" speech, the students felt emboldened by his words since it was a recognition by the most important city politician of the campaign's growing power. This type of public recognition is important, since the reality is that powerful individuals and groups will often not even speak about your group if they don't think it is a threat to their power.

Another incident of an opponent using his words and actions against a campaign was when *Spartans for a World-Class City* put forward a modernization of the city's business tax through a gross receipts tax. The students had become allies with Step Up Silicon Valley, a non-profit created by Catholic Charities, whose goal was to bring together a network of organizations with the goal of reducing poverty in Santa Clara County. The students and Step Up determined that additional funds were needed in order to make San Jose a world-class city. The historical research showed that San Jose was one of the only big cities in California that did not have a gross receipts tax. This led to the students conducting a poll in conjunction with the university's Survey and Policy Research Institute, which showed overwhelming support for a gross receipts tax. At that point, the *Spartans for a World-Class City* and Step Up decided to put forward a ballot measure for the citizens of San Jose to vote on for the November 2016 election. When the media got wind of an upcoming ballot measure, it was a major story in the local newspaper. Soon after, the opponents—which included a major business owner and a top staff member for the mayor—began

putting pressure on Catholic Charities to end their involvement with the campaign. Since these two people were also
board members for Catholic Charities, the executive director decided that Step Up could no longer participate in the
campaign. Clearly, the executive director did not foresee that
his board members would respond with such antipathy for the
gross receipts tax. As for the students, they were not aware that
these two people were even on the board of Catholic Charities,
which the power map, if done correctly, should have uncovered.
Without the support of Catholic Charities, which had given
the campaign a great deal of power, *Spartans for a World-Class
City* decided to agree to a compromise tax increase, which was
a progressive tax that doubled the current business tax, but did
not use a gross receipts tax. With the support of the mayor and
some leading businessmen, a modernization of the business tax
was passed with 65% of the vote.

Assignment

The goal of this exercise is for your group to create a
visual representation of the three parts of your campaign
research (i.e., historical analysis, target analysis, and
power mapping) and a written analysis. Your group will
break into the above three areas. The visual representation might be a poster board, map, photograph, painting,
a board game that expresses the reality in the community,
or some other type of visual representation. Upon completion, these visualizations should be presented. This
will give your group practice using these visualizations to
help explain your campaign to new members. Each of the
three sections should include one to five (or more) members. The below questions guide the visual representation
and written analysis.

Historical Analysis

5.1   Please provide an historical overview of the history of
      your issue. In other words, how has the social problem

played out over time, and what attempts have been made to solve the problem?

5.2   As part of your historical analysis, how has social class, race, and gender affected the history of your issue?

5.3   Which individuals and organizations, both nationally and locally, have been involved in solving your problem both in the past and currently?

5.4   How have groups (both national and locally, past and present) framed your social problem and solution?

5.5   Is your demand and target similar to or different from other individuals and groups who have worked to solve this social problem?

5.6   What side has won or lost over time?

5.7   What have you learned from this historical analysis that will help you get your target to agree with your demands, especially if he or she are lukewarm or opposed to them?

Target Analysis

5.8   Who is your target? (Include a photo of her or him in your visual presentation.)

5.9   What does your target care about? What are her interests?

5.10 What is the political lens that your target sees the world from?

5.11 How might the target's social class, race, and gender affect how he sees the world?

5.12 What is the target's position on your issue, and is it a priority?

5.13 What other policies is your target interested in? Are any of the policies that the target is promoting connected to your issue? If so, how?

5.14 Does it seem like the target is open to changing his mind, and what would need to happen to make this occur?

5.15 Which individuals and organizations does your target listen to?

5.16 What boards does she sit on, and what professional organizations does she belong to?

5.17 How much power does your target have, and where does he derive it from? (You may want to share what you find out with the group that is doing the power map.)

5.18 Under what conditions does the target give in, and how does the target counterattack?

5.19 Is there a secondary target that can pressure or persuade the primary target?

5.20 What have you learned from this target analysis that will help you get your target to agree with your demands, especially if she is lukewarm or opposed to them?

Power Mapping

5.21 How much power does your group possess, and where do you get it from?

5.22 Who are the other stakeholders (both potential allies and opponents) in your community who are concerned about this issue, how much power do they have, and where do they get it from?

5.23 Will your potential opponents actively oppose your demands?

5.24 In light of your group's power and the power of your opponents, do you need more power to win? If not, how might you adjust your recruitment plans to recruit even more members, and if so, what groups might you ally with so as to increase your group's power?

5.25 What have you learned from this power map that will help you get your target to agree with your demands?

Notes

1 Kahn, *Organizing*; Minieri and Gestos, *Rules for Radical Democracy*; Sen, *Stir It Up*.
2 Kim Bobo, Jackie Kendall, and Steve Max, *Organize! Organizing for Social Change: A Manual for Activists in the 1990s* (Washington, DC: Seven Locks Press, 1991); Minieri and Gestos, *Rules for Radical Democracy*; Sen, *Stir It Up*.
3 Minieri and Gestos, *Rules for Radical Democracy*; Sen, *Stir It Up*.

6
STRATEGY AND TACTICS

Tools of the Craft

By the fourth or fifth week of the campaign, your group has been recruiting people by putting up fliers, doing class presentations and tabling, and having people fill out the signup sheets. In your meetings, you have set a positive tone for your group. Your group is also working on its campaign research. Now is the time to take the research that you have conducted and use it to select your group's strategy and tactics.

Strategy

A strategy is the framework and method of a campaign. There are six strategies employed by campaigns, and they include: legislation, policy, alliance building, media and public relations, disruption, and target meetings. When deciding on what strategies to use in your campaign, a group might not select all of the strategies since the more strategies that are employed, the more people you will need to make them successful. The group determines which strategies to use based on whether it will move the target and whether the group has the organizational capacity to carry out the strategy.[1]

Two of the strategies—legislation and policy—focus on what type of change the group desires. Generally, a group runs a campaign to either enact new legislation or to change a policy within an institution. A legislative strategy involves working with a lawmaker, either a student government board member, a city council member, or a state legislator or Congress member, to enact a new law through a legislative body or through a ballot measure to be voted on by citizens. (It should be noted that another way to change the law is through a legal strategy using the court system; however, lawsuits are generally not part of a campus strategy because of the length of time necessary for a court case to be successful.) On the other hand, if the group wants to change a policy within an institution—whether that policy is on campus, or at the city, state, or federal level—the group employs a policy strategy. A policy strategy involves meeting with the individuals and committees that oversee that policy and to make a request for a change based on the facts, evidence, and research. This change might be to improve an administrative system or create a new public program. A policy strategy is best used when the committee is open to input from the public.[2]

Four other strategies—alliance building, media and public education, disruption, and target meetings—are used by campaigns to win demands. Alliance building is used when a group realizes that they cannot win a campaign by themselves, and they need more power to win. Alliance, or coalition, building involves a group working together with other groups—such as labor unions, non-profit organizations, business organizations, and the faith community—for the purpose of winning a campaign. If you decide to pursue an alliance strategy, you will need to discuss with the other organizations how your groups will work together, who will be responsible for what, and how decisions will be made. Be aware that there are grassroots and grasstop organizations, with the former having many leaders and drawing their support from people who are experiencing the issue first-hand, and the latter having one strong leader and drawing their support from charisma or connections to other powerful people. Both types of organizations exist in the community, and both are prospective allies. However, your group will want to discuss what is the right mix of grassroots and grasstop organizations to ally with.[3]

A second strategy is media and public education, which is used to engage the press and social media platforms in order to get out the message of the campaign. By utilizing a media and public education strategy, your group can educate the public about your issue. Your goal is to help frame the issue so that it can be easily understood, is accurate, and portrays your group's work in a sympathetic fashion. At the same time, a campaign may decide that it is necessary to use the strategy of disruption, which is a non-violent public action that disrupts the day-to-day schedule or interferes with the normal operations of the target. Importantly, these three strategies help obtain a meeting with the target, which is the final strategy to be discussed.[4]

Tactics

Each strategy has various tactics or actions associated with it. Tactics are non-violent actions that a group uses to get more power by publicly displaying its strength and to win demands. The goal of any action is to move the target and have her agree to the demands. As discussed above, campaign actions are tied to the various strategies discussed above. For example, a media and public education strategy uses picketing, rallying, marching, street theater, and public hearings to get out its message. A disruption strategy includes walkouts and "takeovers", whether it be an office, building, or street. Target meetings often involve direct negotiations, but they also include a lobby day, an accountability session, or a "day in the life of". If an alliance strategy is employed, your group will work collaboratively with your allies, and all of your actions will be coordinated with them.

Actions Connected to a Media and Public Education Strategy

The actions connected to a media and public education strategy include rallying, marching, picketing, street theater, and public hearings. These actions provide the opportunity for your group to demonstrate its power publicly and to display the skill of its leadership. These actions inform the target and the community that your group has a specific demand, but do not cause the target a great deal of discomfort, so the pressure they apply is in the low to middle range. The hope is that these public events demonstrate the power of the group to the target, the fairness of the group's demands, and the skill of the group's leadership, and that they will lead the target to either agree to the demand or, at a minimum, agree to meet with the group.

Rallying

A rally is designed to inform the target and the community of the campaign's demand and message, and involves meeting at a specific site and includes speakers, chanting, spoken word, and music. A rally generally lasts an hour and sometimes requires a permit, and thus is a legal action. To have a successful rally, it is necessary to have at least ten people; but the more people that attend the rally, the better, as it demonstrates the group's power. At the same time, it is necessary to be realistic about the time it takes to pull off a large rally. It is estimated that it takes at least six months to plan and organize a rally attended by 1,000 people.[5]

Many of my student groups have rallies. For example, *Solar for All* gathered on campus to discuss their plan to introduce state legislation that would subsidize California homeowners to install rooftop solar power by providing rebates to be funded through an oil-extraction fee, which if passed would double the number of rooftop solar units on homes, create 15,000 living-wage jobs in the first year, and decrease the carbon footprint of energy used in California homes by 30% over ten years. Twenty students and community members attended the *Solar for All* rally, but with signs it looked like a lot more. The rally consisted of student and community speakers, and the local press covered the story (Figure 6.1).

Figure 6.1 Saline Chandler, an SJSU student and *Solar for All* member, speaks at a rally.

Marching

Another action aligned with a media and public education strategy is a march. Generally, this action involves marching from one area to another, and the sites are chosen because they have some significance to the issue. Accordingly, the area where your group marches to could be the building where the target works. A march is an exciting event with lots of energy, and it is designed to keep people motivated to continue the campaign and to keep pressure on the target. Generally, a march takes one to two hours and requires at least 20 people. Again, the more people that participate, the better, as more people means more power that is publicly demonstrated. In a march, people carry signs and banners and chant their campaign message. Also, a rally or a statement for the press can occur at the beginning or end of the march.[6]

Some marches require permits from the city, while others do not. You will want to check the campus, city, or state ordinances to determine if your group needs a permit to march. Even if the march does not require a permit, some groups talk to the police and tell them how the march will proceed. For example, when students and community members from the *Gulf Coast Civic Works Project* marched two miles from a baseball stadium, which was built by a New Deal public works project, to the college campus as part of the second anniversary of Hurricane Katrina, the students talked to the police, and the police helped to ensure that the marchers were safe. The press was invited, and the march was the lead story in the San Jose *Mercury News* and on most television stations that night. However, there have been times when students have marched without talking to the police. For example, when the *Students for Racial Equality* marched from the center of campus to the president's office to present their demands, they did not talk to the police beforehand.

Picketing

A third action that is connected to a media and public education strategy is picketing. Picketing involves a line of people walking in a circle, holding signs, and chanting. Generally, a picket takes place close to the building or space where the target works or is currently at. A picket lasts for about an hour and is legal if held on the sidewalk in front of where the picketing is taking place. Your group can also hold a rally before the picket starts, with organized speakers or entertainment. Wherever you choose to picket, you want people who are walking or driving by to see it. The visual of a picket is also attractive to reporters.[7] Interestingly, none of my Social Action students have used picketing as tactic.

Street Theater

A fourth action connected to a media and public education strategy is street theater. Street theater is fun, involves performing a skit of some type, and can involve using props or dressing up in costumes. Generally, street theater is used to dramatize the issue and to mock the target. This form of expression dates back to ancient Greece and was used in morality plays in the Middle Ages and more contemporaneously by social change groups all over the world. An example of street theater is when *United Students Against Sweatshops* (*USAS*) created a mock sweatshop on campus. The mock sweatshop consisted of a large cage that constricted the movement of the students. There were several sewing machines in the "sweatshop", and the students within the cage asked the students outside of the cage to clip off the labels on the back of their shirts and sweaters, so they could use labels to create a quilt that read "No Sweatshops". This quilt was then hand-delivered to their target, the university president, whom the students were trying to convince to join the

Worker's Right Consortium, an organization that ensures that clothes and shoes are not made by sweatshops. This street theater event was covered by the campus press and was covered by the national sweatshop movement. Another student group, *Students for DMH*, held a theatrical event in the overheated Dudley Moorehead Hall, calling on students to faint in the hallways to draw attention to the unbearable conditions in the building. As classes were getting out, and with TV cameras rolling, about 100 students fainted in the hallways. After ten minutes, the students got up and walked through the building chanting that "DMH is too hot" and that it needed air conditioning now. After chanting, the students marched to the president's office, where they attempted to meet with the president. The "faint in" made it on the local Fox News station and on the front page of the campus paper.

In addition, several of my Social Action students have done individual street theater actions. For example, Chris Temblador, or Timbo, a leader of *Students for EOP*, decided to take a bold action before the student government voted on whether to support the demand that the university president rebuild the Equal Opportunity Program, which had been decimated. The night before the meeting, Timbo shaved his head (he had had long, black hair) and phoned his friends to see if they had any handcuffs. The following day at school, Timbo walked around campus with his head shaved and hands cuffed, with tape covering his mouth. His t-shirt read, "Budget Cuts, Fee Hikes, No Student Services, No EOP, No Education". As he walked around campus, people were stunned to see Timbo this way. When a student took interest, Timbo didn't speak—he couldn't as his mouth was taped shut—rather, he just passed out a note asking people to attend that day's board of directors meeting to support the *Students for EOP*'s demand.

Many students were so moved by Timbo's individual act of courage that the board of directors meeting was packed, which most likely helped the board to support the resolution unanimously.

Public Hearings

A public hearing is another action your group can take to educate the public about an issue and to obtain media coverage. There are two types of public hearings: hearings that public agencies sponsor and hearings that a group sponsors by itself. An official public hearing is open to the public and is designed to hear the concerns of the community, so this is a great way for your group to present your demands and influence public policy. At the same time, if your group sponsors a public hearing, and you can get your target to attend, this is a great way to influence the target, and it demonstrates to the community the growing power of your group. However, if the target does not come, your group can still hold a public hearing and have a panel of experts discuss your issue.[8]

The students from the *Gulf Coast Civic Works Project* participated in a public hearing when a state legislator sympathetic to the passage of the federal Gulf Coast Civic Works Act sponsored a public hearing at the university library. Students were provided the opportunity to give formal statements about what they had witnessed and experienced on their trip to the Louisiana and Mississippi. The public hearing received considerable attention in the local and campus newspapers. After the public hearing, the state legislator introduced legislation in the California Assembly, asking the State of California to endorse the legislation. Incredibly, this resolution passed the California Assembly and Senate, and the State of California went on record in support of rebuilding the Gulf Coast through a massive public works project.

Actions Connected to a Disruption Strategy

The main campus actions connected to a disruption strategy are walkouts and occupying spaces. A disruption strategy turns up the pressure on the target, as it involves disrupting the daily life of the target. While my students have rarely needed to use disruption, it is an important strategy to learn since it has been a critical component of social change, especially when the target does not respond to the strategies and actions already mentioned. At the same time, using a disruption strategy comes with risks. First, the target may be so angry about the disruption strategy that he might become less willing to support the group's demands. In addition, some disruption strategies are against the law, and even though the actions are non-violent, the group members risk being arrested. While I teach these types of non-violent civil disobedient strategies, none of my Social Action students have actually used it in a campaign. If they did decide to use civil disobedience in a campaign, I would discuss with them the risks and ensure that it was an individual decision and that they were not being coerced or forced to do it by another group member or community member.

I have had one experience where students chose a disruption strategy, but it was when I was a graduate student, and before I had developed the Social Action class. I was the assistant director of a comprehensive service-learning leadership program at the University of Colorado, Boulder, and a group of students who were in the program were working on a campaign to reverse a tenure decision of a popular Latino faculty member who had been denied tenure by the Rank and Tenure Committee. After using many of the above tactics to no avail, the students decided to go on a hunger strike in the center of campus. Even though the campaign was not part of the program, I talked with them about whether a hunger strike was necessary and how dangerous their proposal was to their own health, but they rejected my advice. The university was unhappy with the service-learning program, as they believed that the program was behind the students' actions. The director of the program was called into a meeting with university administrators, and he told them that this was not the case, that the students were acting independently, and that the program had told the students to not proceed with their hunger strike. However, the students proceeded, and after several days of the hunger strike, and with the national media descending on the campus, the chancellor of the university intervened and said she would consider the demands of the students to reverse the Rank and Tenure Committee's decision. With the intervention of the chancellor, the students suspended their hunger strike. Eventually, the students won their demand, as the chancellor overturned the Committee's decision, and the professor was granted tenure. The service-learning leadership program continued on and is now in its 26th year of operation.

Walkouts

Students throughout the United States have used walkouts as a way to effect social change. In Los Angeles, Latino high school students walked out of class in the famous "blowouts" of 1968 to protest unequal education. More recently, after the November, 2016, election victory of Donald Trump, college and high school students across the nation walked out of classes to encourage their schools to become sanctuary spaces in order to protect undocumented students from possible deportation.[9] A walkout is a powerful action since you are sending the message that the issue you are concerned about is more important than the education that is occurring in the classroom. A walkout disrupts the normal flow of the day on a campus and can put pressure on the target to respond to the demands, particularly if the target is a college president or other campus administrator. While none of the groups in Social Action have used a walkout, several of my students who have taken this course have used it while on campus. In one instance, several former Social Action students called upon students to walk out of their classes in support of lecturers that were going to be let go due to budget cuts. One of the students, Roberto Garcia-Ceballos, decided to use a megaphone in the hallways. The police were less than thrilled with this decision, and they asked him to stop. Roberto was insistent and continued to use the megaphone to encourage students to walk out of their classes. This caused the police to chase Roberto through the hallways. Looking back on it now it is funny, but at the time it seemed quite serious.

Occupying Spaces

Another action connected to a disruption strategy is to occupy a space. The space occupied might be an office, building, street, or public park. Taking over a public space disrupts the daily flow of life, and it is most effective if the target is directly affected by the occupation. The amount of people necessary to conduct this type of action depends on the type of occupation. A small group can occupy an office, while a larger group is needed to occupy a building, and an even larger group is necessary to occupy a street or public park. Occupations are generally considered when the previous actions discussed have failed to move the target to meet the group's demands. It is important to recognize that an occupation is illegal and might lead to arrest. And while the time spent in jail may not be long, the campus administration may take disciplinary action as well. Thus, great thought must be put into this type of action. At the same time, occupying space is an important part of the legacy of civil disobedience, when people have felt that there is such a need for social change that they risk being arrested to promote their demands. This type of non-violent action dates back to Thoreau's seminal article "Civil Disobedience", and has been used successfully by autoworkers in the sit-down strikes in the 1930s and by civil rights workers in the 1960s to desegregate lunch counters and to hire Black workers. More recently, college students have used occupations of offices (e.g., the campus president's office) and university buildings to convince universities to pay campus janitors more money, to not use sweatshop labor to make university apparel, and to stop tuition increases. The most famous image of these student occupations was the University of California at Davis occupation of a campus pathway. In the fall of 2011, students had occupied a paved path in support of the Occupy Movement that had started in New York as a response to the corrupting influence of money in politics. The UC Davis students were instructed to clear the path by campus police, and when the students did not disperse, the police sprayed them with pepper spray. Video of this action went viral on the internet, which led to worldwide outrage and ultimately led to the firing of the police officer who pepper-sprayed the students and to a compensation package of $30,000 to each of the 21 students sprayed.[10] My Social Action students have never occupied a space illegally. The *Gulf Coast Civic Works Project* and *Students for Racial Justice* both considered it, and the latter group did decide to hold a one-hour occupation of Tower Hall where the president's office sits, but they did so with the campus administration's approval (Figure 6.2).

Figure 6.2 Rogelio Garcia from *Students for Racial Justice* speaks at the occupation of Tower Hall.

Actions Connected to Target Meetings

The actions connected to the strategy of meeting with the target include direct negotiation with the target, a lobby day, an accountability session, and a "day in the life of". These actions range from low to high pressure and are designed to demonstrate to the target the power and leadership of the group and to move the target to meet the demands.

Direct Negotiation With the Target

Whether your group is advocating for a new law or a modification of a policy within an institution, the strategy of direct negotiation with the target is key. The objective of this strategy is to obtain a meeting with the target so the group can make a direct appeal to the decision-maker. When the campaign starts, it may be difficult to obtain such a meeting with the target, as the issue might not seem important enough to her, or the target doesn't want to deal with this issue. However, as the group begins to implement the other strategies (e.g., public education and media), the target will hopefully begin to understand that your group is serious about the issue, and you will not be going away. At some point in the campaign, the target will hopefully be convinced to grant a meeting with the group. When this happens, your group should spend time preparing for the target meeting as if it were any other event and think through the various components of the meeting.

The group needs to decide on who should attend (generally from three to six people), how the meeting should unfold, who should speak and who should make "the ask", what should be the tone, where should the target and group members sit, where should the meeting be held, and what demand, if any, the group is willing to abandon in exchange for a more important demand to be met. At the meeting, the group should do its best to control the space, by deciding where people sit and how they address the target. Importantly, the group should do a practice meeting beforehand, with someone playing the target. Remember, the goal of the meeting is to convince the target to support the new law or policy that your group is proposing. To achieve this goal, your group may decide that the right tone is strong and firm, so the pressure applied to the target might stay at the low to medium range, or your group may decide to be angry and confrontational, which could raise the pressure on the target to a high level. Or you may want to have a group member play a "bad cop" (i.e., angry) and a "good cop" (i.e., calming the bad cop). This allows for the target to experience the passion of the group, but also its reasonableness.[11]

At this initial meeting, or soon after, it is possible for the target to agree to your demands. In my work with student groups, the target has agreed to support the demands early on in a campaign in several cases. For example, one week after *Students for Racial Justice* held their kickoff event that received local, national, and international media attention, the president asked the Tower Foundation board member who made the racist statement to step down, as well as the academic vice president who said nothing in the meeting when the racist statement was made. However, if the target does not respond positively, it is time to apply more heat by writing letters, signing petitions, and making phone calls to the target. Again, if the target does not respond, the heat is turned up higher, with the group perhaps leading marches, pickets, and rallies. Again, if the target does not meet the demands, more heat is applied by taking further actions, which might include street theater, accountability sessions, or walkouts. If still no positive response, a boycott or non-violent office takeover could be organized. It has been my experience that targets generally meet the demands if the above steps are taken, particularly if the demand is commonsensical and reasonable and is supported by many students and the community. After more heat has been applied, the target may ask for another meeting, or may decide to say yes to the demands without even meeting with the group.

It has been my experience that the student campaigns have generally been able to obtain target meetings. *Students for DMH* were able to get a meeting with the campus provost about getting air conditioning, *Students Against Sweatshops* met with the university president to ask him to sign on to the Worker's Rights Consortium, and *Campus Alliance for Economic Justice* met with a majority of the city council members to ask them to vote in favor of raising the minimum wage by $2 instead of sending it to the ballot. The first two target meetings led to victories, while the latter meeting was unsuccessful at changing a majority of the city council members' position.

Students for Campus Safety's target meeting also led to the winning of their demands. Before their meeting with their target, which was the university police chief, *Students for Campus Safety* met to decide what they were going to say, who was going to say what, and where they would sit. On this last point, the group decided to not let the police chief sit at the end of the table, as this is where the person in control sat, and rather have one of the student leaders take that sit. When Natasha, one of the student leaders, took this "power" seat, the police chief looked stunned and sat down in one of the chairs along the long table. The students had made their point. The students wanted to convey that they were powerful and that they were not going to be run over by "the people in charge". Within a few months, the police chief met all three of the group's demands, and the students believe that this small act of taking the chair played a role in his decision. It was the students' demonstration of organizational power along with their knowledge of the issue—which was discussed in the last chapter—that proved decisive in this campaign.

At a target meeting, some unexpected things can take place. After meeting with several lower staff members, the *Students for Racial Equality* obtained a meeting with the university president. The night before the meeting, the students spent several hours preparing for the meeting, and the following morning they printed out a nice agenda for the president and his staff. The students arrived one-hour early to discuss final plans for the meeting. As part of the meeting, they asked several professors, including me, to be there to witness the meeting and to provide support if the president unjustly attacked them. The students had taken their seats when the president's chief of staff entered the room. When she saw that three professors were sitting around the edge of the main table, she informed the students that the professors would have to leave if the meeting was to happen. The students said, "No, the professors are staying, since they are our mentors." They also informed the chief of staff that they would be conducting the meeting, and not the professors. The chief of staff responded that the students were acting as possible puppets of the faculty, which led to some heated words between the faculty and the chief of staff. The faculty explained that the students were adults and that it was an outrage to say that the faculty were using and controlling the students. In addition, a faculty member told the chief of staff that she had been in this same room several years before with a previous president, where students along with faculty had met to discuss racial injustices on the campus. In the middle of this exchange, the president of the university walked in. The chief of staff told the president that the meeting was not going to happen because of the faculty's presence, and the president, on command, turned and walked out of the meeting. With this target meeting canceled, the students decided to call for a press conference, which led to the president agreeing to most all of the students' demands.

One note of caution: the more important the target is, the more difficult it will be to get a meeting directly with him. "Important people" have many layers of aides to protect them from the public. So while it is important to do everything possible to get a meeting with the target, it is sometimes very difficult. The *Gulf Coast Civic Works* campaign found this out when they were trying to get a meeting with the chairperson of the Committee on Homeland Security, Congressman Bennie Thompson. The students wanted a meeting with Congressman Thompson, who was from Mississippi, since they believed that if he co-sponsored the legislation, he could help enact the public works legislation. After numerous failed attempts to set up a meeting with Congressman Thompson, the students flew to Denver, Colorado, for the Democratic National Convention in 2008 to meet with him and other Congress members. Incredibly, the open environment of the national convention, where Congress members were accessible before and after events, made it possible to meet with Congressman Thompson. After one meeting, the *Gulf Coast Civic Works* campaign got to ask him directly if he would be willing to co-sponsor the legislation. He immediately said yes, and he directed the students to go talk to his aide, whom he pointed to, so as to inform the aide of his decision. They had similar interactions with several other Congress members and left the convention with the belief that they had to continue to look for creative ways to meet with targets since it was a critical part of getting them to say yes. In addition, the students working on the *Gulf Coast Civic Works* campaign desperately tried to get a meeting with President-Elect Obama. The campaign even had the two community organizers from the Gulf Coast who had provided the then Senator Obama with a tour of the devastation of Hurricane Katrina to write a letter asking for a meeting. President-Elect Obama and his staff never responded to this request. The campaign then tried to meet with Speaker of the House Nancy Pelosi, and the students did get a meeting with several of her key staff members, but couldn't get a meeting with her either.

Lobby Day

Another action connected to the strategy of meeting with the target is a lobby day. The primary goal of a lobby day is to convince the targets of your demands, but a secondary goal is to get press and to develop leadership skills. A lobby day generally requires ten to 40 (or more) people who travel to city hall, the state capitol, or the nation's capitol to meet with legislators. While the group always wants to meet with legislators who are from their districts, there may be certain legislators who are considered critical to pass the policy that the group is promoting. These legislators become targets, and research needs to be conducted on them. Generally, a lobby day includes a rally or press conference beforehand in front of city hall or the state capitol, followed by meetings with the legislators. In preparation for a lobby day, all of the previous skills of preparing for and organizing a rally and target meeting should be followed. And remember, legislators expect to be contacted by their constituents, so go into the meeting with the belief that you are helping them do their job, as they need the information you possess to make good decisions.[12]

The *Gulf Coast Civic Works Project* conducted a lobby day with Congress members at the nation's capitol. Meetings were set up with Gulf Coast Congress members, as well as members from the Congressional Black Caucus, and with the office of the Chair of the Labor and Education Committee, where the bill was sent and languishing. In addition, the *Gulf Coast Civic Works Project* co-sponsored a lunchtime event at the Capitol for congressional staff members, where people from the Gulf Coast spoke about the hardships created by Hurricane Katrina.

Accountability Session

An additional action connected to the strategy of meeting with the target is an accountability session. An accountability session takes a small group to plan, but it takes a large group to execute. The idea is to invite the target to meet group members and their allies in a room filled to capacity. At the meeting, your group and allies present information to the target about your issue. The highlight of the meeting is when you ask the question: will the target support your demands? The hope is that, by making the case for the demands in front of a large number of people present who also support the demands, the target will feel the pressure and say yes to the demand. As with all target meetings, preparation is necessary to determine what questions should be asked, who should ask them, and what should be the tone. It should be noted that an accountability session, which the media is invited to, is considered an action that puts medium to high pressure on the target, since people in power generally do not like to answer questions publicly, especially if the questions come from a powerfully organized group that is demanding something and that are witnessed by a large crowd.[13] Unfortunately, none of my Social Action students have used this tactic.

A "Day in the Life of"

A final action connected to the strategy of meeting with the target is a "day in the life of". This type of event involves asking the target to walk around for a day and experience the issue first-hand. What is powerful about this action is that it can help the target understand the reality surrounding the issue in a profound and deep way. The hope is that by seeing and learning about the issue, and getting the opportunity to discuss the issue with people who are affected by it, the event can change the mind of the target and move him toward supporting the group's demand.

A "day in the life of" is an action that puts low to medium pressure on the target, since the group is trying to get the target to support the demand by learning about the issue more deeply.[14] None of my social action groups have used this approach, but my Social Action students that sleep out in solidarity with the homeless each year have convinced a city council member to sleep out with them to experience what it is like to sleep outside in the cold.

Assignment

6.1   Your group should choose two to five strategies to employ for your campaign. Does your research from Chapter 5 (i.e, historical and target analyses, and power map) provide insights into your strategies? As part of your analysis, explore what are the strengths and weaknesses of the strategies chosen. In addition, explain that tactics you have chosen to use that are connected to each strategy. Then, choose one tactic and write up a plan on how to implement it. Please provide an in-depth plan on how the action will unfold on the day it is held, and the pre-planning that needs to occur, including who will be responsible for carrying out each part of the plan.

Notes

1   Minieri and Gestos, *Rules for Radical Democracy*; Sen, *Stir It Up*.
2   Minieri and Gestos, *Rules for Radical Democracy*; Sen, *Stir It Up*.
3   Aleyet Hines, "Top 5 Tips for Being a Grasstops Organizing Rockstar," Change University, http://change-university.com/rockstar (accessed March 31, 2017).
4   Minieri and Gestos, *Rules for Radical Democracy*.
5   Minieri and Gestos, *Rules for Radical Democracy*; Work Group for Community Health and Development, "Community Tool Box," University of Kansas, http://ctb.ku.edu/en/table-of-contents/advocacy/direct-action/public-demonstrations/main (accessed March 31, 2017).
6   Minieri and Gestos, *Rules for Radical Democracy*; Work Group for Community Health and Development, "Community Tool Box".
7   Minieri and Gestos, *Rules for Radical Democracy*; Work Group for Community Health and Development, "Community Tool Box".
8   Bobo, Kendell, and Max, *Organize!*; Minieri and Gestos, *Rules for Radical Democracy*; Work Group for Community Health and Development, "Community Tool Box".

9 Reuters, "Thousands of Anti-Trump Protesters Take to the Streets," November 10, 2016, www.cnbc.com/2016/11/09/thousands-protest-across-us-over-trumps-shock-election-win.html (accessed April 6, 2017).

10 Joe Garofoli, "UC Davis Pepper-Spray Officer Awarded $38,000," *SF Gate*, April 16, 2015, www.sfgate.com/politics/joegarofoli/article/UC-Davis-pepper-spray-officer-awarded-38-000-4920773.php (accessed April 6, 2017).

11 Kahn, *Organizing*; Minieri and Gestos, *Rules for Radical Democracy*.

12 Minieri and Gestos, *Rules for Radical Democracy*; Work Group for Community Health and Development, "Community Tool Box".

13 Bobo, Kendell, and Max, *Organize!*; Minieri and Gestos, *Rules for Radical Democracy*.

14 Minieri and Gestos, *Rules for Radical Democracy*.

7

CAMPAIGN KICKOFF

Going Public With the Media

By the beginning of the second month of the campaign, your group has chosen your strategies and tactics, and your group continues to recruit (i.e., the fliers are up, tabling and class presentations have been on-going, and people are filling out the signup sheets. You have also begun holding meetings for the newcomers, and you have given these new folks something small but meaningful to do. It's now time to begin planning your kickoff event, which publicly announces that your campaign has begun. Please note that if you are continuing a campaign from the previous semester, or have joined a community campaign, your group has probably had its kickoff event. However, there are still lessons for you to learn from this chapter, so read on.

Campaign Message

As you prepare for your campaign kickoff, your group should develop a campaign message. A campaign message is based on the values of your group and communicates these values to your base of supporters, the media, and the target. Core values of a group might include the principles of fairness, equality, democracy, or ethical practices. Moreover, a campaign message is factually accurate, it is clear and concise, it provides information to support the assertions made, and people who are trusted on the topic deliver it. Lastly, the campaign message is delivered repeatedly.[1]

An example of a good campaign message was *CAFÉ J*'s message to raise San Jose's minimum wage from $8 to $10 an hour. Whenever students and allies were asked about the minimum-wage campaign, they would state the below three points of the campaign message, and they would conclude by asking people to vote for the ballot measure. The minimum-wage campaign's message was the following:

1. If you work hard and play by the rules, you deserve a fair wage.
2. $8 is not fair since a full-time minimum-wage worker can't pay for the basics on that salary.
3. Increasing the minimum wage encourages self-sufficiency and reduces the need for government services.

First, as stated above, a campaign message is built on the values of the group. The group's primary value was fairness, as can be seen in the first statement: "If you work hard and play by the rules, you deserve a fair wage." Most Americans and San Joseans agree with the idea that hard work deserves a fair way, so it was a great way to start the campaign message. A secondary value was self-sufficiency, and while people in the group believed in this principle, it was also chosen as a way to broaden the appeal of the minimum wage increase to conservatives. Second, a campaign message is factually accurate. If your group is to be seen as credible, your message must be true. Again, this is where your research will be extremely helpful. With the minimum-wage campaign, we could demonstrate to most San Joseans that $8 an hour was not fair since full-time minimum-wage workers couldn't even pay for the rent in Silicon Valley on that salary.

It also made sense to most people that this low pay would then force workers on to government services. The accuracy of the message helped to attract more supporters, and it played well in the media. More importantly, it led the target—in this case the voters of San Jose—to overwhelmingly agree with the demand.

Third, your campaign message must be clear and concise. We are bombarded daily with tons of information, and your audience will not remember, nor do they have time for, a long, drawn-out message. Thus, your campaign message must be crisp and to the point and should not be long. Clearly, the three points of the minimum-wage campaign are clear, concise and to the point. Fourth, your message provides information to support the assertions made. Note that the minimum-wage campaign's message logically moves people from the principle of fairness to then show how the $8 minimum wage is not fair based on the facts and then demonstrate how this low wage undermines another principle held near and dear to Americans. Lastly, the message was delivered by people the community trusted the most on this issue: a non-profit leader heading up the largest anti-poverty program and the CEO of United Way, as well as by the students.

It should be noted that the Raise the Wage coalition, which was composed of *CAFÉ J* and labor, non-profit, and faith communities, had conducted a scientific poll of San Jose voters focusing on what points were the most convincing to raise the minimum wage. The three points that San Jose voters gave the highest approval ratings to (over 70% agreed) were the three points that were chosen to be the campaign message. The students and allies agreed on this campaign message because why talk about something that had 50% approval rating when they could talk about a point that had over 70% approval rating. Thus, when students and allies were asked about research that showed that the minimum wage increased unemployment, the students and allies would say they had research that showed that this wasn't the case, but then would state, "But the real issue is . . ." and go on to state one, two, or all three points of the campaign message. In this way, the campaign did not lose focus and was always on message. At the same time, I realize that it may be difficult to conduct a scientific poll due to a lack of funds. However, it is still possible to develop a series of points for your campaign message and to do an informal poll with the larger audience, asking them which points are the most convincing. The results of this "straw poll" can be used to develop a powerful campaign message that is repeated over and over.

Lastly, while a campaign message is similar to an organizational rap in that it explains your issue and offers a solution, a campaign message is different in that it is what you focus on continually when talking to the public; it is the three or four points your group keeps repeating over and over.

Planning the Kickoff Event

The kickoff event informs the campus (and perhaps the city, state, or nation) that your group has officially begun the campaign. At a kickoff event, your group publicly announces the demands, you specify who the target is, and you make it clear that you are asking your target to say yes to your demands. Where you hold the event and how the event unfolds is critical. The event should be held near to where the target is located, so it is clear that you are delivering a message to her. The press likes an event that is visual; the more visual the event, the more likely the press will cover it. It is also important that the kickoff event is well planned, powerful, and demonstrates that the group has the leadership skills necessary to win the campaign.

The kickoff event should generate as much interest and excitement for your campaign as possible. Thus, you need to get your supporters and the media to this kickoff event. To achieve the goal of getting as many people as possible to the event, your group will want to utilize several tools, including fliers and social media—which were already discussed in Chapter 4—as well as a "commitment card", press release, and the use of dry-erase boards.

Commitment Card

A commitment card is a more sophisticated way to get folks to sign up to come to an event, as it is more individualized than just writing down your name, since it gives a person the opportunity to make a small commitment to the campaign. A commitment card has the name of the event on it, a place for the person to sign and to commit to coming, and a space to give their contact information. A commitment card is effective because it gives you something concrete to ask people to do when tabling or after a classroom presentation.

Figure 7.1 is an example of the commitment card used to attract students to sleep out for Poverty Under the Stars. Notice that there are two parts to the card, both of them filled out by the student, but the group keeps one half, and the person who filled it out keeps the other half, as this helps to remind her what she signed up for.

As important as it is to get students to sign a commitment card, it is equally as important that you use the card to remind people of the upcoming event. A week before the event, email and text the people that have signed the commitment cards in order to remind them to attend the event. Three days before the event, email and text them again and say that you are excited to see them at the upcoming event. The day before the event, call the people and remind them to come. This technique has been extremely successful for student groups to attract larger number of students (over 100) to attend the event.

Campus Sleep Out Commitment Card

12th Annual Poverty Under the Stars

Thursday, November 16, 2017
Smith and Carlos Statues

I agree to: ____come to the 7-10 pm event, _____sleep out at the event, ____bring a tent

Commitment Signature: _____

Bring a sleeping bag and pillow!
If you have questions about the event, contact Dr. Myers-Lipton at smlipton@gmail.com

Sponsored by Cesar Chavez Community Action Center and Community Change Concentration (SISS Dept.)

-----------------------------------TEAR HERE---

Campus Sleep Out Commitment Card

12th Annual Poverty Under the Stars

Name: _____

Email: _____

Phone: _____

I agree to: _____come to the 7-10 pm event, ____sleep out at the event, ____bring a tent

Figure 7.1 Commitment card for Poverty Under the Stars.

Dry-Erase Boards

Another tool to attract a large crowd to your kickoff event, as well as to your other activities, is to write on the dry-erase board or chalkboard a note stating the activity, as well as the time and place. You should put "Please Save" underneath the time and place of the event, as well as use erasable markers. Do not use permanent markers, as they do not erase, and this will get your group into trouble for permanently marking the dry-erase board.

Media Relations Plan

For your campaign kickoff, your group needs to develop a media plan in order to get as much press as possible. Your media plan for this kickoff event should be part of your media and public relations strategy. And while the media plan is fun to develop, it also can bring more power to your group and help you win your demands. To implement your media plan, choose one or two people to head up the *media relations team*. While many folks will help with media relations, these one to two students will put extra thought into how to involve the media in your campaign, will make sure that the media is always being considered during meetings, and will oversee the media plan's implementation.

The media relations plan includes a step-by-step approach to working with the media. The first thing to do is to develop a list of media contacts. This list should include people in the student and local newspapers, the mainstream TV and radio stations, and the alternative media (ethnic newspapers and TV stations, and community blogs). As part of developing this list, reach out to each of these media outlets and ask for the phone number and emails of the assignment desk. At newspapers and TV/radio stations, the assignment desk is the place where the decision is made whether to cover your story. Generally, any time you call a TV or radio station or newspaper asking them to cover an event, you will ask to talk to the assignment desk.

In addition, start collecting a list of the names of newspaper reporters that cover your area and topic. Reporters need to get the approval of the assignment desk, but they can make the case for the paper or TV station to cover your story. In the beginning, you will have little idea of the various reporters.

However, by the end of the campaign the media team will most likely know most of the reporters covering your issue. Don't be surprised if the reporters ask your group to contact them when you have something "in the hopper" or if the reporters call your group asking for your thoughts about a certain story they are writing about.

For the campaign kickoff, your group will also want to create a press release. A press release is a statement that educates the media about your event. The press release follows a certain format, with the words FOR IMMEDIATE RELEASE on the top left and then your group's media contacts. Below this is the title of the press release (capped) and possibly a subtitle (uncapped), followed by the city and state, with the text of the press release after that. The opening lines of the text state the who, what, where, and when of the event. The next lines provide the demands and some historical overview. The press release ends with four number signs (#), which indicate that there is no more text.

The student groups' experience with the media has been mostly positive, with the reporters generally doing their best to tell the story fairly and accurately. Of course, you will still need to work hard to make sure that your campaign message is clear and that your story is compelling.

Day of the Event

In addition to recruiting people to the kickoff event and enacting a media relations plan, your group needs to decide what is going to happen at the event, and who is going to do what. This requires developing an agenda for the day and includes such things as who is going to speak, what will the group's signs say, and who will be recruiting as people walk by. Your group should have a speaker state the problem, another speaker state the solution (i.e., the demands), and perhaps another speaker to ask the target to respond. With so many things to do, the kickoff event provides your group with a great opportunity for shared leadership and democratic participation.

For the event, a podium is a good prop, as it gives the proceedings some gravitas. Most college campuses have podiums, and they are available through the president's office or some other campus office. However, you can also use a music stand. A podium or music stand helps focus people's attention on the area where the event is occurring and serves as a place to hang a sign or to place microphones from the media. Behind the speakers, it is good to have ten or more supporters holding large signs, as this shows that your group is united, and it is a good visual for the media.

On the day of the event, the media team should assign several students to be greeters for the reporters or cameramen. The greeters should welcome the press to the event and introduce group members that are available for comments. The student groups have found that it is good to provide the media with a copy of the speeches that are to be given. This ensures that the quotes in the paper will be accurate. Of course, your group will want to get the contact information of the reporters, and this information should be logged into your media contact list.

At the end of the event, you may want to have a speaker state what the next event is. Also, your speakers should actively recruit students, encouraging them to go over to where the folks with the signup sheets or commitment cards are and to fill one out. You may also have a specific action for them to do, like call or email the target. After the event, evaluate your kickoff event. This evaluation is done a day or two after the event, explores how effective the event was, and includes an analysis of how successful the recruitment and media relations plans were.

All of the tools described above can be used for other types of events as well. Press releases and contacting the assignment desks can be utilized in all future events when you want the media to attend. Commitment cards can also be used to ask students and community members to make a commitment to support the campaign (e.g., to vote "yes" on the issue), as well as to sign up for various campaign activities. Figure 7.2 is an example of this type of commitment card:

COMMITMENT CARD: Spartans for a World Class City

___ I will vote **YES** on the retooling of the business tax if it is to be on the November ballot.

   ___ I need more information

___ I will volunteer in the campaign. I would like to (mark all that apply):

    ☐ Attend our meetings
    ☐ I would like to participate in the poll on November 18-22nd by volunteering for:
       ☐ one shift: **1 ½ hours**
       ☐ two shifts: **3 hours**
       ☐ three shifts or more!
    ☐ Table at noon and talk to other students about our campaign

Please Print- *Standard text messaging rates will apply for text updates. To opt out of text updates, check here:* ☐

Name: _____ Cell Phone: _____

Email: _____

Figure 7.2 Commitment card for *Spartans for a World Class City*.

Case Studies

At the *Students for Racial Equality*'s kickoff event (Figure 7.3), the students held a press conference, where they publicly stated the problem, announced their demands, and called on the university president to respond. In addition, the students announced there would be a non-violent action directed toward the president if their demands were not met.

At the conclusion of this event, the students walked over to the president's office, which was 100 yards away, and attempted to deliver their demands personally to him. When the president

Figure 7.3 Students for Racial Equality students Estelia Velasquez (foreground) and Christina Salim (background) being interviewed by the media before the start of their kickoff event.

refused to meet with the students, they posted the demands on his door, à la Martin Luther, who posted his 95 theses on the Wittenberg church door in 1517. All major news outlets covered this story, and it was even picked up by Fox News, the *Huffington Post*, and the *Daily Mail* in England. When reflecting upon the campaign, Estelia—who was a member of the media relations team—commented on how empowering the kickoff event was for her:

> My favorite action that my group did was the press conference because we were so nervous that no one was going to show up. We did not know what we were doing, of course there were some mistakes we made along the way, but we got our message across which was important. I loved that we had so many supporters who believed in what we were doing. The fact two members and myself got the media there was an accomplishment. We were not sure that we were going to get the media there. We had some news channels tell us they were coming but others did not confirm, and when we had them show up we were ecstatic. I definitely enjoyed the press conference. We left with a sense of accomplishment that we got the attention we did. After this press conference, we had lots of phone calls from reporters wanting to interview us.

The below press release was written by *Students for Racial Equality* and was sent to radio and TV stations and the local and campus newspapers:

For Immediate Release
Media Contact

Estelia: (408) 924–1000, Estelia@gmail.com
Luis: (408) 924–1000, Luis@gmail.com

ANOTHER SJSU RACIST INCIDENT
Tower Foundation Board Member Makes Racial Slur

SAN JOSE, CA—On Monday, November 10 at 11:30 am, *Students for Racial Equality* will hold a press conference at the Smith and Carlos Statues to discuss the most recent racist incident at San José State University, and our request for immediate action on this issue.

The racist incident occurred in the Spring of 2014 when a board member of the Tower Foundation—which is SJSU's philanthropy organization—stated during a meeting with university staff: "I contribute to this University because these little Latinas do not have the DNA to be successful." A member of President Qayoumi's cabinet was present and remained silent. Soon after the incident, a Latina staff member who was present at the meeting made an informal complaint, but when the University took no action, she made a formal complaint through the University's protocol. As a result of the formal complaint, SJSU conducted its investigation this semester, but no results have been reported.

This incident adds to the growing issue of San Jose State University's inability to address issues of diversity appropriately and shows a continued lack of leadership and inaction from this administration.

Students for Racial Equality DEMAND:

1. To have the removal of this Tower Foundation board member;
2. We request a letter of apology from the VP to the complainant;
3. Students for Racial Equality calls for mandatory anti-racism trainings for administration, faculty, staff, and students and urges the implementation of protocols for cabinet members to respond to racist incidents with strict consequences for those who allow racist comments to go unreported.

####

Below, Estelia describes her actions leading up to the kickoff event:

> Our media strategy used a press release to get the media's attention. Yessenia, a fellow group member, and I wrote up the press release. We showed it to the Social Action professor to get his ideas as well. We worked on the press release for about a week or so and ensured that it was good enough to send out to the different media outlets. After we found the contact information for the media contacts, we had to spend a fair amount of time making calls and sending emails to ensure that the press was going to show up to our press conference. You have to be persistent if you want the media to really take notice and find a date and time that will ensure that you get the media's attention.
>
> Our first media contact that we made came out of nowhere. Yessenia and I were walking by the library when someone from Univision was on campus interviewing people on an issue, so we gave him an interview and off camera we gave him a brief statement on our issue. He was intrigued by what we were doing so we then exchanged information. When you see someone in the media, I highly recommend that you go and talk to him or her and get their contact information because you never know when you may need to contact them.

CAFÉ J, another student group, held a kickoff event (Figure 7.4) to publicly announce that the minimum-wage campaign in San Jose had officially begun, and the students and their allies were about to begin collecting signatures to put a $2 increase on the ballot. Up to this point, the students were working behind the scenes, meeting with members of the non-profit and labor

Figure 7.4 Leila McCabe from *CAFÉ J* announcing the launch of the minimum-wage campaign using a podium.

communities, and conducting a poll to demonstrate the viability of the campaign. At the press conference, student, non-profit, and labor leaders spoke. Several television stations (e.g., ABC and Univision) covered the event, as well as the San Jose *Mercury News*. The newspaper article led with the title "A Reasonable Wage Increase Sought", which *CAFÉ J* was pleased with since it made the demand to increase the minimum wage to $10 seem reasonable.

The *Gulf Coast Civic Works Project* held their kickoff event in the entrance hall of the MLK Library on campus. Under banners of Dr. Martin Luther King, the students announced that they were initiating a campaign to enact legislation to create 100,000 public works jobs for the people of the Gulf Coast as a response to Hurricane Katrina. Over 100 people attended, and

ABC and CBS radio stations, Fox News, and the San Jose *Mercury News* covered the event. In order to maximize the number of attendees, the students contacted a senior center right across the street, and they brought over 30 elders. In addition, two similar kickoff events occurred on the same day; one event was held at the New Orleans federal building and was led by the NAACP Gulf Coast Advocacy Center, and the other was held at Jefferson Davis Community College in Biloxi, Mississippi, and was led by faculty and students. WLOX (the only TV news station in the city) and the *Sun Herald* (the only large newspaper in the city) covered the Biloxi kickoff event. This three-city kickoff was extremely important, as it showed that the students were supported by people in the Gulf Coast and were not loose cannons.

Assignment

7.1   To prepare for your campaign kickoff, your group needs to develop a campaign message. The group should choose the values that the campaign will be based upon and choose three or four statements that are factually accurate, clear and concise, and provide support to the assertions made.

7.2   For the kickoff event, your group needs to create a flier, commitment card, and press release. In addition, your group needs to write up a *media relations plan*. Your plan should include the following: (a) the names of one to two people to head the media relations team; (b) a list of the local media assignment desks and their contact information; (c) a list of reporters and their contact information; (d) a summary of who will email the press release to the media, who will put up the fliers, and who will recruit students to the event using the commitment card; (e) who will reach out to the media a week out, three days out, and on the morning of the event; (f) who will greet the media on the day of the event; (g) who will be master of ceremonies at the event; and (h) who will speak.

7.3 After the kickoff event takes place, answer the following questions about your kickoff event:

   a. Were you successful at attracting a large turnout of supporters?

   b. Were the commitment cards and fliers helpful in attracting a large turnout?

   c. How many commitment cards did you get signed, and how many came to the event?

   d. How effective were you at recruiting new members because of the kickoff event?

   e. Did the media plan work to attract a large turnout from the media?

   f. Analyze how much press you received and whether your message get delivered (i.e., to the target, to possible supporters, to the public)? Did the target "receive" the message?

   g. How did the event go?

   h. What were the positives and challenges of the event?

   i. What did you learn for future events? At your next event, what would you do similarly and differently?

Note

1 Wellstone Action, *Politics the Wellstone Way: How to Elect Progressive Candidates and Win on Issues* (Minneapolis, MN: University of Minnesota Press, 2005).

8

GROUP DYNAMICS

Ensuring the Group Doesn't Implode

Your group should be planning the kickoff event, and your recruitment and media relations teams are up and running. At this point, your group has been meeting regularly, and you've had many individual conversations with your group members about the campaign. In addition, your recruitment team is continually building your base of support. It is now time to take a moment to reflect on your group dynamics. At first, you may think group dynamics is a side point of the campaign; however, group interaction plays a fundamental role in whether the student groups win or lose their campaigns. Group dynamics can create such a strain on the group that, when done poorly, it becomes nearly impossible to get anything else done in the campaign. Thus, it is extremely important that your group pays attention to how it is interacting with each other.

The main place for your group interactions will be at meetings, which are probably taking place in a classroom, dorm room, or coffee shop. During these meetings, it is critical that your group pays attention to every aspect of *how* the group meets: how the meeting starts, who is leading or facilitating the meeting, who talks during the meeting, how interruptions are dealt with, how decisions are made, and whether people are respectful and are actively listening to each other. For the meetings, your group should promote interactions that encourage people to give their ideas and perspectives, to listen to one another, to not say things that put down other members, and to follow through on what they say they are going to do. In order to have this type of group interaction, I suggest that a student facilitates the meeting and that this position is rotated for each meeting. The facilitator can be chosen in many ways, but generally students just voluntarily put their names forward to be a facilitator. Many times, the student has an interest in the topic that is to be discussed that day. Importantly, the facilitator attempts to guide the conversation by making sure everyone is heard. It is also important that the facilitator doesn't control the conversation. If the facilitator has something to say about the topic, he should step down at that point and hand over the facilitation to another group member. In addition, it is necessary that different students facilitate each meeting so as not to concentrate power in the hands of one or two students. Leila, from the *Campus Alliance for Economic Justice* (*CAFÉ J*), reflects on her group's dynamics and their struggle to create a non-hierarchical group:

> We had a lot of discussions on what we wanted our group to look like and how we wanted to run it. There was talk about either a hierarchical top-down leadership or a more horizontal leadership. In the beginning, we definitely worked more horizontally. We all made decisions together, and no one was named as the leader of the group. We even rotated facilitators at meetings so that no one person led the group all the time. This became more and more

challenging especially when we started to grow our coalition. It also becomes a bit more confusing when the group gets more attention. We are used to working in a top-down environment and people want to know who the leader of a group is.

If you are using this book for a course, decide if you are going to meet outside of your classroom, and if so, where and at what time you will be meeting. I recommend that your group meets at least once every two weeks at a minimum outside of the classroom, since this will allow your group to include the people that you are recruiting. At these group meetings, you might want to ask your members to bring food, as this always encourages students to come to a meeting. And while good meetings are rewarding, make sure that your group doesn't get stuck in meeting mode. You want to have good meetings so that your actions will be successful at moving your target to agree to your demands.[1]

Roles of the Facilitator

The facilitator has many important roles. First, the facilitator creates the agenda for the meeting. A week before the group meets, the facilitator should ask the group for input for the agenda (i.e., what items need be discussed). After receiving this input, the facilitator should send the draft agenda to the group at least 24 hours before the meeting. At the beginning of the meeting, the facilitator should ask the group if they have any last-minute additions to the agenda. If there are additions, these can be put at the end of the agenda and will be discussed if there is time. If there is not enough time, these agenda items will be discussed at the next meeting. If it is an urgent item, the facilitator might ask the group if she can move it to today's agenda.

Another role of the facilitator is to keep the meeting moving. As part of this role, the facilitator explains each item, calls on group members to respond to the item, and, if necessary, facilitates the group decision-making process (more on decision-making later). To help keep the meeting moving, the facilitator may want to give a certain amount of time for each agenda item. This helps ensure the meeting is not spent on one agenda item. If time runs out for an agenda item, then the facilitator can ask the group if they want to give five, ten, or 15 more minutes to the item, with the group deciding. Clearly, the facilitator is someone who stimulates and guides the discussion, but without being overbearing and autocratic, and straightforwardly moves the group from one item to the next on the agenda.

An additional key responsibility of the facilitator is to promote positive group interactions. The facilitator ensures that people respond to each item and that there is a full discussion of them. At the same time, the facilitator is watching to make sure that the same one or two people are not always talking or that the same group of people is not always quiet. If the same students are silent, or there are only one or two people talking, the facilitator can suggest that he would like to hear from more folks in the room, particularly the people that have not spoken. If this doesn't work, the facilitator can nicely name some of the quiet students, saying something like, "It would sure be great to hear from Amanda, Jose, or Anna."

If one or two people continue to dominate the discussion, the facilitator can use one of the following "tricks of the trade" to help encourage more equal group participation. First, the facilitator can call for a "go around", where everyone speaks for a maximum of one to two minutes about the topic. If you have a group of ten, this will take ten to 20 minutes, but it allows for everyone to speak and ensures that not just one or two people are talking or that a large part of the group is not silent. Another strategy to equalize group participation is to give each group member (except the facilitator) two or three sticks or matches, with each stick or match worth one, two, or three minutes' worth of speaking time (the facilitator or the group can decide which works best for your group). If a student speaks, she discards one of the matches or sticks. Thus, each person can only speak three times, which will help ensure that many group members are contributing to the discussion. If the lack of talking or domination by a few continue to be issues, the facilitator can do a fun exercise. The facilitator can bring out a large ball of string, and when anyone speaks, the person takes the string and then throws it to the next person who speaks. Each time a person finishes speaking, she throws it to the next person who wants to speak. This process provides a visual representation of your group interactions. It shows visually and powerfully who is speaking, and who is not. At the conclusion of the meeting, or 30 to 40 minutes into the discussion, the facilitator should lead a discussion about what the string pattern says about your group interactions and discuss ways to make sure that all are participating more equally.

The facilitator also ensures that hurtful words and actions are not being used in the group. Few people like to be in a group where put-downs occur, and it is the facilitator's role to help create a safe environment where all feel comfortable. (Of course, it is also up to the whole group to create a safe environment, but the facilitator is in a leadership role, so it is important that they do their best to provide a safe environment.) To achieve this end, the facilitator should continually monitor the feelings of the group and group members. If the mood turns negative, and people start saying hurtful things, the facilitator can ask people to re-phrase their negative comments and put them in a way where people can hear their concerns. The facilitator can also remind people that the group is committed to providing a safe environment where all people feel comfortable. She also might remind people to speak in "I" statements, as these are less hurtful and confrontational. Instead of a group member stating, "You all never do anything for the group," the facilitator might ask the person to re-phrase it in a way that the group can hear the concern; thus, the facilitator might suggest something like, "I feel anger and frustration when members don't complete their tasks for the group." This suggestion promotes good group dynamics since the first way is accusatory and probably not accurate (since "never" is most likely a generalization), while the second allows for the person to express their feelings, but without the others feeling blamed. Also, there might be a good reason for the group members not to get something done. This latter way allows for the conversation to focus on the concern, rather than on the blame, and will more easily allow for a solution, which might be a new group rule, such as when someone can't complete a task that they say they are going to do, they will let the group know, and the group will see if another person can do it.[2]

One other strategy that the facilitator can employ to ensure good dynamics is to ask someone to serve as a vibes watcher, which is someone who watches for the feeling and mood of the group and makes comments to the group when he feels that the group dynamics are becoming too negative. The vibes watcher might offer suggestions, as well as ask group members to comment on how to improve the vibe in the room. Of course, the vibes watcher can also state that the vibe in the room is positive and uplifting. In addition to a vibes watcher, the facilitator should ask someone to serve as a note-taker, since it is helpful to have a record of what took place at each meeting to refer to in the future or for group members who have missed the meeting for some reason.

Up to this point, I have focused on the facilitator's role when students speak too much, too little, or in a way that harms the group dynamics. However, another role of the facilitator is to help members become active listeners, so as to really hear what is being said. To encourage this, the facilitator might ask all group members to have three seconds of silence after a group member speaks to ensure that people are not just trying to get in the next word as fast as they can, which, of course, leads to not hearing what is being said, since the next speaker is worrying about getting his point across. In addition, the facilitator can model good listening by restating what she heard a person say in the group (e.g., "So what I heard you say is . . ."), which shows the group that what is being said is being listened to and seen as important. Finally, the facilitator can remind the group that talking to someone else while a group member is talking is not conducive to positive group dynamics as it is tough to listen when a side conversation is going on. Also, the facilitator can remind them that body language is important and that if a person rolls his eyes when someone makes a point, or has his arms closed off, that this body language is not helpful for a positive group process.

A further role of the facilitator is to help the group make decisions. Not all agenda items require a decision, but for the ones that do, there needs to be a clear, transparent, and democratic way to choose between various options. The two most common ways that groups make decisions is by voting with the majority ruling, or by consensus. Generally, groups do not run well if one or just a few people are making the decisions. The only time that a small subset of the group should make a group decision is when there is not time for all the group members to meet to discuss the question at hand, and this group has been empowered by the larger group to make such a decision. However, at the next meeting, this small group needs to let the larger group know what decision was made and how it came to the decision. For most group decisions, the group will either vote or use consensus. Voting is easy, as most students are accustomed to it. Just as in voting during an election, when there is a decision to be made, everyone gets one vote, and one option or proposal wins out over the other by securing a majority of the votes (i.e., 50% plus one). Voting is generally used when the decision is not critical to the group, such as when deciding about what day a certain event will take place. Voting is also used when you have a limited time to make a decision. Majority rule through voting is a quick and easy way to make decisions, as there is a proposal on the table, and people either say either "yeah" or "nay". So if you are limited for time, voting is probably your best method. However, the downside of voting is that it is a win–lose situation, and the people who lose the vote may feel like their voice is not being heard. Thus, the facilitator needs to ask the members of the "losing" group if they feel like their voices were heard. If people don't feel heard, group members will become frustrated and eventually leave the group.[3]

The other way to make a group decision is through consensus. Consensus decision-making is used when the group decision is extremely important to the group *and* you have enough time, since this process can take an hour or two. Consensus is seen as a win–win method of decision-making, and it operates in the following matter:

• A proposal is put forward to resolve some problem, or an idea is put forward about how to move forward.

- The proposal is amended, changed, and modified through discussion as people offer creative alternatives. It is also possible to synthesize various ideas in the proposal. At the same time, if an alternative leads to a dead end, it can be withdrawn.

- After discussing the proposal and the modifications, the facilitator asks if anyone has objections or reservations. If people don't have reservations, the facilitator can ask if they have reached consensus, which can be done through a show of hands or by raising your thumb up. If all hands or thumbs are up, then consensus has been reached and the decision has been made. If not all hands or thumbs are up, the facilitator might ask the group to discuss further modifications to satisfy the reservations.

- Another strategy the facilitator can employ is to ask the people with reservations to express their objections and then still move forward by offering: (1) non-support (e.g., "I don't see the need for this, but I will go along"), (2) reservations (e.g., "I think this may be a mistake, but I can live it"), or (3) to stand aside (e.g., "I personally can't do this, but I won't stop others from doing it"). However, if a person is strongly opposed, or morally opposed, and cannot support the proposal, then the person can block consensus, and the group must go back to the proposal stage.[4]

Whether your group chooses consensus or voting, or chooses consensus for the most important decisions and voting for all other decisions, the main thing is that you need to use one of these decision-making strategies since it allows for the whole group to express their ideas and does not impose the will of a few on the whole group. Lucila Ortiz from *Collective Voices for Undocumented Students* discusses how the group's decision-making skills helped her group be successful. Lucila states:

> Our group was very intentional about how decisions were taken. It was discussed in one of our first meetings that we all had to be in agreement in order to move something forward. At first, this seemed to me like an impossible task, but I was surprised to see how much agreement we all had. We ended up having no problems making decisions and we were all very happy with the end product of our campaign.

And Rochelle Jackson-Smarr from the *Student Homeless Alliance* notes: "We worked very much democratically. We all had to agree on a decision before moving forward. For the most part we worked together really well."

Culture of Accountability

One of the biggest issues that a group needs to deal with is accountability. Sometimes, a group member states he is going to do something, and then he doesn't do it. If this member continues to not do what he says he is going to do, or other members are not doing what they say they are going to do, this will create incredible frustration in the group and will lead to negative group dynamics. Therefore, I recommend that your group creates a culture of accountability. This culture of accountability starts with people doing what they say they are going to do. To encourage a culture of accountability, the facilitator should go through the assignments for the week and hear from each member about what she did and did not do. This provides public pressure on the person to complete the task. If being gently called out does not do the trick, the group may want to have a discussion about everyone completing the work they take on for the group. Also, the group may ask a professor or staff person to talk to the individuals who are not doing their fair share of the work. Whatever you do, don't let this continue in silence; it must be dealt with up front and in a cordial fashion.

If the above advice is followed, your group may have Estelia's experience with *Students for Racial Equality*. Estelia states:

> The one thing that I liked about my group is that we all shared the power. There was not one person that made the final decision, as we all made it together. We decided to do this because it was important in how the group would get along, and no one had to feel like their opinions did not matter. We all wanted to hear what each member had to say to figure out how to make whatever we were discussing work. And this worked out very well because no one in the group felt like they were not being heard. We all got along great, which helped us in moving forward in our campaign.

Assignment

8.1   Up to now, how has your group handled the facilitation of the meetings? Has a facilitator been used? How have they been selected? Has someone made an agenda? Has the same person facilitated the meeting? Have the group interactions been positive? If not, why not? Have you used any of the ideas from the text to help you improve your group dynamics?

8.2   For the next meeting, select a facilitator. To get in the habit of creating an agenda, make the agenda together as a group. People should offer their suggestions about what should be talked about at this upcoming meeting. The facilitator will then take this information and create the order of the agenda. After the conclusion of this next meeting, the group should give the facilitator feedback. I recommend that you create an evaluation form that can be filled out by the group members based on whether the facilitator created a clear agenda, the meeting kept moving, there were positive group interactions, decisions were made efficiently and soundly, and people were held accountable. The evaluation form might also have a question focusing on areas of improvement for next time. This evaluation form is extremely helpful in providing information to the facilitator about how the facilitation went and how to improve their facilitation skills. Describe how the evaluation of the facilitators went.

8.3 In order to explore how members of your group are currently feeling about the group dynamics, the group will do an experience called "Strike a Pose". This exercise involves everyone striking a pose that represents how people feel about the group and its interactions. What you do with your hands, feet, facial expression, and location to the other people in the room will give your group a visual representation of how people feel about the group interactions. To start the exercise, allow the group members 30 seconds or a minute to strike a pose. This exercise is done in complete silence. After people have struck a pose, have them look around the room and notice where people are and what they are doing. Then, have a facilitator lead a discussion to debrief this exercise. Importantly, people should be asked why they are in that location and why they struck the pose that they did. Also, what does this exercise say about the group dynamics? What is going well, and what are the challenges? How might this information help your group dynamics?

8.4   Discuss with your group what makes for a good or bad decision. Has your decision-making process been easy or problematic? What decision-making process will your group use (consensus, voting, and/or small group decides)? How is this decision-making process working for your group?

Notes

1   Minieri and Gestos, *Rules for Radical Democracy.*
2   Tova Green, Peter Woodrow, and Fran Peavey, *Insight and Action: How to Discover and Support a Life of Integrity and Commitment to Change* (Gabriola Island, BC, Canada: New Society Publishers, 1994).
3   Rocky Mountain Peace Center, *Communities of Conversation and Action.*
4   Rocky Mountain Peace Center, *Communities of Conversation and Action.*

9
CAMPAIGN PLAN

Keeping It on Track

By now your group is in its final planning stages for your kick off event (or you have had the event), and you may have even started to plan for your next action. Now it is time to develop your entire campaign plan and begin to implement it. The campaign plan is important since it ensures that everyone is on the same page regarding where your group is going, what it needs to do and when, and how to get there. Thus, the campaign plan is the basis for all your future actions. Furthermore, the campaign plan will be extremely helpful for the future students who might work on this campaign in the following academic term. The actual implementation of the campaign plan will proceed until the end of the semester and perhaps beyond.

So far your group has identified an issue (i.e., created one to three quantifiable demands and identified a target), developed an organizational rap, implemented a recruitment plan, created a media relations team, conducted research (historical analysis, target analysis, and power map), and chosen your strategies and tactics. You will want to put all of these things into your campaign plan. In addition, a campaign plan includes a timeline that includes "turning up the heat" on your target; a fundraising

plan (if necessary); and eventually an evaluation of the implementation of the campaign. I would obtain a large three-ringed
binder and then make a section for each of the above areas. You
can organize it the way you like, but here is my recommendation:

1. Issue identification (i.e., discussion of the specific demands
   and how the target was identified)
2. Recruitment plan
3. Media relations
4. Research (historical analysis, target analysis, and power map)
5. Strategy and tactics
6. Timeline
7. Fundraising
8. Implementation: actions conducted
9. Evaluation of campaign

Let us turn our attention to each section of the campaign plan.

Previous Work

Your group has already completed most of the work for the first
five sections, so it just means taking what you have already done
and putting it formally into the campaign notebook. You may
have to update certain sections. For example, you may want to
add to the list the names of various reporters whom you have
recently connected with.

Timeline

A campaign needs to have a timeline to guide its actions,
which involves estimating how long it will take to win the
campaign. Of course, the end date for the campaign is just an
estimate since it is difficult to know in the middle of a campaign when victory might occur. Also, the end date can be
changed anytime the group believes it is necessary to do so.

However, it is important to have this date in mind because it can be used to plan out the steps it will take to win the campaign. The beginning date of the campaign is the kickoff event, with today's date also included. The rest of the timeline is filled in with actions that the group will take to win the campaign. In Chapter 6, your group has already planned two actions. It is now time to think through a series of actions, besides the action you have already developed, which will lead your group to victory.

When putting these actions into the timeline, it is helpful to consider the pressure you are applying to the target like the metaphor of a burner on an oven. As you know, a burner starts off at a low temperature, but can, if necessary, be raised to higher and higher temperatures. Campaign actions are similar to this. In the beginning of the campaign, your actions start off at a "low heat" (i.e., less confrontational). I recommend that in the opening phase of the campaign that your group should be firm and strong, but not confrontational. It is true you are upset about the injustice at hand, but I suggest that you come across as being reasonable and not too hostile. Many times, I recommend that the group should assume the best from your target; perhaps your target has not acted to solve the problem because she doesn't have enough information or because she is misinformed. During this early part of a campaign, you may even ask for a meeting with the target to provide her with information. However, as the campaign progresses, and more actions are taken and more pressure applied, your attitude toward the target may harden and your language may become more forceful. As you continue with your actions, three things can happen. The first possibility is that the target agrees to meet your demands, and your group wins the campaign. The second possibility is that your group is in the middle of the campaign and the academic term ends. The third possibility is your group decides that the target will never agree to the demand, and you decide to end the campaign. Later in the chapter, I will discuss these three possibilities in greater depth.

Implementation

Once the campaign plan is completed, it is time to implement it. The implementation mainly focuses on the actions that your group has agreed upon to get your target to agree to your demands. These actions should be clearly laid out in your campaign plan, and they move from lower to higher heat.

As you move forward to implementing your campaign plan, it might be good to review the qualities of a good leader discussed in Chapter 2. In addition, the below three qualities will also help your implementation plan be successful:

1. **Stay focused**. You need to be singled-minded about your campaign. As stated earlier, it is important not to get distracted. You already have school work, possibly a job, and other responsibilities that take your time. Thus, limit other activities. Of course, your group may go and support the work of other student campaigns at an event if you are using this book for a class, but be aware that you need to keep focused on your campaign if you are to be successful, so guard your time wisely.
2. **Engage in actions regularly**. Actions keep members involved. There will always be some turnover in campaign as people come and go. However, by engaging in meaningful actions, the members of your group will feel more connected to the campaign and are more likely to stick around, even after the academic term ends.
3. **Stay up to date on your issue**. Read the newspaper, go to meetings where your issue is discussed, continue doing research, and follow what your target is saying and doing.[1]

Fundraising

One final component of a campaign plan is fundraising. Some campaigns don't need to fundraise, while others may need money for some aspect of the campaign. A good place to get money is from the university itself. Some colleges have funds available for official student groups, which can be used for food or t-shirts. Your group can also hold fundraising events. Students from *CAFÉ J* raised several hundred dollars by selling coffee and food for their scientific poll. Later in the campaign, *CAFÉ J* students ran a "money bomb" fundraiser, which gathered ten students at the Cross-Cultural Center and over the course of the night, the students made phone calls to their friends and families asking them to make a donation to the campaign, giving people until midnight to make a donation. This "money bomb" was success-ful at raising over $1,000 in a brief amount of time. *Students for DMH* raised over $100 by appealing directly to students asking them to donate $1 to help in their effort to bring air condition-ing to the building. Another great way to raise money is to do an "-a-thon". It could be a serve-a-thon at a local non-profit, a walk-a-thon, or a golf-a-thon. On some level, it doesn't really matter what the activity is. The main thing is that group mem-bers get pledges from their family and friends to do something over a short period of time (four to eight hours). People can make an hourly pledge (e.g., $1 an hour; if the person does six hours of the activity, the donation is $6), or a pledge just at a flat rate (e.g., a $10 donation). Students using the "-a-thon" method can generally raise over $500 a person.

If the group has a need to raise money continually, you might want to create a fundraising committee. At the minimum, some-one needs to keep track of the money raised and be accountable for it. It is extremely important that you use the money only for the campaign. It is also important that the group decides col-lectively how to use the money. When money is involved, it is important to have a high level of integrity. If the money is kept track of appropriately and used wisely, your group's status will rise.

Concluding the Campaign

As discussed earlier, as the campaign progresses, three things can happen. First, the group wins its demands; if this happens, the campaign is over, as your group has won the campaign, and it is time to start planning the victory party. At the same time, if the group has three demands, and the target agrees to only one or two of the demands, the group will need to decide on whether to continue fighting for the other demands. To win a campaign, it might take one week, one year, or seven years. As stated earlier, *Students for Racial Equality* won their main demand of removing the board member from the Tower Foundation in less than one week after their kickoff event. After pushing for another two months, *Students for Racial Equality* won their second demand when the university president apologized to the Latina who heard the racist comment and made the formal complaint. However, they did not win their third demand, and the group lost steam between the semester break, and the group eventually dissolved. Similarly, *Every 15 Minutes a Student Waits* won their demand for more printers in the main library after a one-month campaign. However, it took two years for *CAFÉ J* to win the $2 increase in San Jose's minimum wage, and it took three years for *Students for DMH* to win their demand for air conditioning in Dudley Moorehead Hall. Incredibly, it took seven years for *Students Against Sweatshops* to get the university president to sign an executive order creating a sweatshop-free campus.

As stated above, if you win the campaign, the next step is a victory party. Your group should invite all of your members, allies, and people that helped on the campaign. It is important to enjoy your success since it takes a great deal of energy to win a campaign, and the people that played a role in this victory should be recognized. Interestingly, the target might not give any credit to your group because when a group is victorious, it actually encourages other groups to demand change as well, which is something that many powerful people want to minimize. However, the victory party is not the end. After the party, the group should stay active to ensure that the demand is actually put into practice. Too many demands have been won, but never implemented. Thus, the group must monitor the implementation of the demands. If the group does win the campaign, you may decide to stick together to take on another issue. Campaigns are similar to playing poker. When you win in poker, you get a few more chips to play in the next round, which is the same as in a campaign. By winning, your group will have gained "some chips" to play in the "game" of politics.

A second possibility is the academic term ends and your group is in the middle of its campaign. If this happens, your group might continue the campaign outside of the class or co-curricular structure. However, I never put this expectation on my students. If the students want to continue the campaign outside of the class, I tell them that it is up to them. Of course, if there are no group members who want to continue the campaign, the group may decide to give a short presentation during the first week of class to the next group of students with the hope that three or more people will step forward and choose this issue, and continue the campaign.

A third possibility is your group decides that the target will never agree to the demand, even after your group has raised the heat to high levels. At this point, you may decide to end the campaign. This is a difficult step to take, as it is a recognition that your group has lost the campaign, and no one likes to lose, especially when you have put so much time and effort into the campaign. However, even when a group loses a campaign, something else might develop out of the ashes. This happened in the *Gulf Coast Civic Works Project*. Even though the student group helped to create two federal bills, had them introduced into Congress, got 43 Congress members to co-sponsor the bill, and then helped lead a coalition of 200 organizations across the nation to enact it, the students and their allies could still not even get a hearing or a vote on the bill, as it languished in the Education and Labor Committee in the House of Representatives. After four years of fighting for a public works project in the Gulf Coast, the students and allies came to the conclusion that they did not have enough power to change the minds of President Bush or President Obama, nor could they change the minds of the Democratic leaders in the Senate or House of Representatives. With that realization, the students decided to end their campaign. However, on a retreat to decide what they should do next, the students decided to focus their work locally, and they changed their name to *CAFÉ J* and then started a minimum-wage campaign, which led to a huge victory two years later. In fact, the skills and leadership developed in the *Gulf Coast Civic Works Project* provided them with the necessary skills to win this next campaign.

Assignment

9.1   Your group needs to create a campaign plan and put it into the campaign notebook. So far, your group has identified an issue (i.e., created one to three quantifiable demands, identified a target), developed an organizational rap, implemented a recruitment plan, created a media relations team, conducted research (historical analysis, target analysis, and power map), and chosen your strategies and actions. You will want to put all of these areas of the campaign into a notebook. In addition, you will now add the following sections to your campaign notebook: a timeline and a series of actions to "turn up the heat". The timeline needs to have an estimate of how long you think it will take to win the campaign, and designs of various actions you want to take over the course of the campaign. The timeline also includes the end date on the far right of a large piece of paper, and the date of the kickoff event and today's date on the far left of the paper. Then, work backwards from the end date towards the present and put in the actions (e.g., tactics, recruitment, media relations) that your group believes will be needed to win the campaign, with the month and week represented. After your group has completed the timeline, include it in your campaign notebook. Remember, your actions at the beginning of the campaign should be at "low heat" (i.e., less confrontational). Please note that this timeline is a working document and should be updated as the campaign proceeds.

9.2 Write up your campaign message, making sure you succinctly state the problem, offer a solution, and describe the actions to solve the problem. You may want to update your organizational rap and include the campaign message in it.

9.3 Have your group discuss whether you need to raise funds, and if so, how much. If your group does need to raise money, check with the student government to see if there are funds available for student groups. In addition, discuss with your group which of the above ideas (i.e., making direct appeals to students and family, an "-a-thon", money bomb, or selling donuts or coffee, etc.) seems the most appropriate for your group. Then, write up a fundraising plan and include it in the campaign notebook.

Note

1   Minieri and Gestos, *Rules for Radical Democracy*.

10

EVALUATION

PASSING IT ON

When the campaign ends, or at the end of the academic term, a campaign evaluation is completed. If the campaign ended during the term because the group won or lost, the evaluation provides important information for social action campaigns to be undertaken by future students. If the campaign is on-going, then you and the group will also be writing the evaluation for the next group who may decide to continue the campaign in the following academic term.

There are nine areas that compose a campaign evaluation, and they include an analysis of issue identification, recruitment, research, media outreach, group dynamics, leadership, strategy and tactics, campaign implementation, and lessons learned. More specifically, you and the group will evaluate the following topics:

- **Issue identification**. Discuss your demands (e.g., were they specific enough?), whether you chose the right target, and whether you maintained the desire to fight for this issue throughout the campaign.
- **Recruitment**. Examine how successful your group was in recruiting new members, as well as what were your most and least successful recruitment plans, and why. Also, you

will want to explore how many new members you recruited (i.e., leaders, workers, paper members), and what changes you recommend to make the recruitment process even more successful.

- **Research**. Explore whether your historical analysis, target analysis, and power map proved to be accurate. You should also discuss how this research helped your campaign and explore what else your group could have done to improve on the research.

- **Media outreach**. Discuss how successful you were at getting the media to your events, as well as what were your most and least successful media events, and why. You will also want to highlight the relationship you built with reporters, discuss how these relationships helped your campaign, and explore what changes you recommend to improve on the media outreach.

- **Group dynamics**. Examine how the group dealt with group dynamics (e.g., if students were too dominant, or didn't talk enough). Your group should discuss what your group did to encourage members to share in the group tasks and whether it worked or not. Your group should also explore how well your group made decisions and whether voting or consensus worked better. Moreover, your group should discuss how well your group resolved conflicts.

- **Leadership**. Explore how "leadership" played out in your group. Looking back, did your group follow a traditional definition of leadership or the newer definition offered? Also, discuss what leadership qualities and skills you developed in the campaign and what qualities and skills you would like to develop in the future.

- **Strategies and tactics**. Discuss how your target responded to the strategy and tactics that you utilized in the campaign. Did the target respond in the way you expected or differently? If your group won, discuss why the strategy and tactics you chose were so effective. If your group lost, discuss why the strategy and tactics you chose were not effective. If the campaign is still on-going, discuss what other strategy and tactics might move the target.

- **Campaign implementation**. Explain how well your group executed the campaign and what, if anything, you could have done better. Importantly, how well did your campaign build power and capacity? Did your campaign message bring in more members and allies? You will also want to explore what obstacles got in your way and how your group overcome these obstacles, as well as whether your campaign message brought in more members and allies.

- **Lessons learned**. Reflect on what were the lessons learned from the campaign. If your group won or lost the campaign, what are the major lessons for future social action campaigns? If the campaign is not complete, and with the possibility of it being continued next academic term, what are five recommendations you can provide to a future group who might pick up the campaign?

Assignment

Based on the above nine areas, you and the group will write up an evaluation to be placed in the campaign notebook. In addition, your group will design a 20- to 25-minute presentation of the evaluation. This presentation might be a skit, a lecture, a PowerPoint presentation, or any other presentation format you'd like. As with all campaign activities, the evaluation should be in-depth, involve all group members, and demonstrate creativity.

11
THE HERO'S AND SHERO'S JOURNEY

This book started in Plato's Cave, and it ends with the hero's and shero's journey. Recall, Plato's Cave tells the story of a person moving out of ignorance and towards knowledge and wisdom, and then after seeing reality clearly, the story discusses what happens when the person returns to the cave to talk to people. The reason I started the book in Plato's Cave is that this is the condition in which many Athenians lived (allegorically) in the 4th century BCE, and it may well be the condition of many Americans in the 21st century. Similarly, the hero's and shero's journey provides a step-by-step map to move out of ignorance and towards wisdom, self-discovery, empowerment, and ultimately personal and social liberation.

The hero's journey is based in the work of Joseph Campbell, the 20th-century mythologist, who discovered that cultures across the globe had a similar myth about how humans, in order to become fully human, go through a series of experiences. Campbell called these experiences the hero's journey, which he laid out in his book *The Hero With a Thousand Faces*. Americans are familiar with this journey because it has been used in many major blockbuster movies, including *Star Wars*, *Harry Potter*, *Indiana Jones*, *The Matrix*, *Shrek*, *Finding Nemo*, *Lord of the Rings*, and many more.[1]

In all of the above movies, the following series of events occur:

- The hero is living in the ordinary world, unaware of what is about to unfold.
- The main character receives a call to adventure.
- The shero refuses the call to adventure.
- The hero has a meeting with a mentor, who has special knowledge for the hero.
- The protagonist crosses a threshold and enters into a new, strange world, where the values and rules are different than the world she knows.
- The shero is tested and discovers who are her allies and enemies.
- The hero prepares for a large challenge in this new world.
- The central character faces her greatest fear and perhaps even death.
- After facing death, the shero obtains the treasure she has been searching for.
- The hero completes the adventure by leaving this special world—generally in a chase scene—with the treasure. In this scene, the hero is tested with death one final time.
- The protagonist then returns home with the treasure, which generally has some power to help, heal, or change the world for better, just as the shero has been changed for the better.[2]

Any of the above movies could be selected to demonstrate the hero's journey, but this book will examine the books of *Harry Potter*. In the first book, *Harry Potter and the Sorcerer's Stone*, Harry is an ordinary 11-year-old-boy living with his Aunt Petunia and Uncle Vernon, and he knows nothing of the magical world or that he is a wizard. Sadly, Harry's ordinary world is a cruel one, where his aunt and uncle mistreat him often. Harry's call to adventure comes when Hagrid, the Keeper of Keys and

Grounds at Hogwarts, delivers a letter to Harry inviting him to attend the school. Harry moves to the next stage immediately, which is the refusal of the call to adventure, when he responds to Hagrid, "No, you have made a mistake. I can't be a wizard. I mean, I am just Harry, just Harry." The next step on the hero's journey is to meet a mentor who has special knowledge. At Hogwarts, Harry meets his main mentor, Albus Dumbledore, who provides Harry with special knowledge giving Harry his father's invisibility cloak and by showing him how Tom Riddle becomes Voldemort by looking into the Pensieve. The next step is to cross a threshold and enter a strange, new world, and Harry does this in the beginning of almost every book. For example, he experiences a new world when he enters the wizarding world in Diagon Alley, when he enters the world of the Mermish in the second task of the Triwizard Championship, or when Hermione, Ron, and Harry leave Hogwarts to look for horcruxes around England. Of course, Harry is tested in all the books, such as when he has to overcome Dolores Umbridge's tortuous black quill, or when Severus Snape tries to humiliate Harry in Potions class. In addition, Harry prepares for the challenges he is to face when he practices spells for the Triwizard Championship, or when he is trying to learn occlumency from Snape. Harry also goes through the stage of facing fear and death in all the books, generally when he is fighting against Voldemort. After facing death, Harry obtains the treasure he has been searching for, such as the Sorcerer's Stone, the Triwizard Cup, or the elder wand. Of course, Harry generally leaves the special world with the treasure after a final battle with Voldemort, and the last scenes of the books are generally ones of peace and calm, as Harry returns home with the treasure (i.e., the Deathly Hallows), with the world and himself transformed for the better.[3]

Harry Potter went through the hero's journey, but all of us must go on it. My hope is that the campaign has been a hero's and shero's adventure. In the campaign, it is my hope that you accepted a call to adventure and that you found a mentor who had special knowledge of the social conditions surrounding your issue and how to bring about social change. In this campaign you may have been tested, and you needed to figure out who were your allies and opponents. Perhaps you needed to prepare, and you had to face your fear (e.g., public speaking, or taking a position that your friends and family disagree with). And while some organizers face the fear of death, none of my students have faced this in their organizing. Yet, an experience that my students have experienced is obtaining the treasure that they had been searching for, as they come away with a win in their campaign. I have witnessed my students receiving recognition, such as plaques, crystal glass awards, and commendations from the State of California. More importantly, the students have "returned home" by making their community better, while at the same time they have been transformed as they have become better critical thinkers, have obtained a deeper understanding of diversity, and have become empowered to undertake a life-time of social change.

It is my belief that the hero's and shero's journey provide insights for social change agents. In summary, these insights include:

- **Most of us see ourselves as ordinary folks living in an ordinary world**. In general, most of us are going to school, working, and taking care of our family responsibilities, and we feel good about these ordinary but important tasks.
- **There is something not right in the world, and through something you have seen or heard, you have become aware of it**. This sentiment is best summed up in *The Matrix*, when Morpheus tells Neo, "You're here because you know

something. What you know you can't explain, but you feel it. You've felt it your entire life, that there's something wrong with the world. You don't know what it is, but it's there, like a splinter in your mind, driving you mad." Just like Neo, you have become aware that there is something wrong in the world.[4]

- **Be open to the call to adventure.** The call may come in the form of a new class, an internship, travel, or a new job. When the call of adventure comes, your first response may be to turn it down. Be open to the call, and eventually answer the call that makes the most sense to you.

- **Find a mentor.** Learn the special knowledge she or he has about the issue or social change.

- **Prepare yourself.** On this journey, you will be tested, so prepare yourself emotionally, spiritually, and physically for this community change work.

- **Learn who your allies and opponents are.** Some might appear as friends but turn out to be opponents, while some might appear as opponents but turn out to be allies.

- **Be aware that some social change agents do face fear and death.** You very well may face fear in your campaign, as you may need to overcome your apprehension of giving a TV interview or talking to some important politician. And while your college Social Action campaign will not endanger your life, some change agents do face death, so it is important to consider what you are willing to sacrifice for. As Dr. Martin Luther King stated, "If a man has not discovered something that he will die for, he isn't fit to live."[5]

- **Whether you win or lose your campaign, be aware that there is individual and social transformation occurring.** If you obtain the treasure and win your campaign, you will be changed individually and help bring about a better world.

You Are the Chosen One

There is one more thing about the hero's and shero's journey, and it is perhaps the most important part of the adventure. Generally, I end my Social Action class with these words: YOU ARE THE CHOSEN ONE. This gets to the heart of this social change work: that what we do as individuals matter and that our life-story is important. We have to break the chains in Plato's Cave and begin our journey toward wisdom and empowerment. We are called to do what Harry Potter does in *The Half-Blood Prince*, and announce, "I am the chosen one." This is what President Obama meant when he stated:

> Change will not come if we wait for some other person or some other time. We are the ones we've been waiting for. We are the change that we seek. . . . We are the hope of the future; the answer to the cynics who tell us our house must stand divided; that we cannot come together; that we cannot remake this world as it should be.

So it is up to you and to me, and to all of us, to heal our nation and repair the world.[6]

This self-realization that it is up to you, and not someone else, and that each of us is on our own hero's and shero's journey is critical, as it is will empower you to continue in this work over the long-term and to endure the setbacks and temporary losses that are all part of the journey. Cornel West, the great American philosopher, argues that we don't need sprinters, but long-distance runners who are committed to work for justice throughout their entire lives.[7] My hope is that this book has given you the knowledge and skills to be successful not just in the campaign you have been involved with, but for the rest of your life in our democracy.

Assignment

Complete the below questions raised by Plato's Cave and the hero's and shero's journey:

11.1   What are the similarities between Plato's Cave and *The Matrix*? (You may need to watch the opening scene of *The Matrix* to answer this question.) Are we in the Cave and Matrix today?

11.2   What, if anything, has led you to believe that "there is something wrong with the world"?

11.3   Have you received "the call to adventure"? If so, what form did the call take? If not, why don't you think you have received it yet?

11.4   If you have received the call, did you accept it or refuse it?

11.5   Is there a person within your network who can serve as your mentor? If not, where can you find her or him?

11.6   What do you need to do to prepare yourself for this journey?

11.7   What is a fear that you need to overcome to be successful on this journey?

11.8   What "treasure" would you most like to bring back to your community?

11.9   Do you agree with Joseph Campbell that we are all invited to be on a hero's or shero's journey? Explain. What are the implications of this for your life?

Notes

1   Richard Camp, "How a Common Hollywood Screenwriting Technique Can Transform Your Marketing—Part 2 of 3: The Hero's Journey," January 9, 2015, https://campcreative.net/blog/common-hollywood-screenwriting-technique-can-transform-marketing-part-2-3-heros-journey (accessed April 17, 2017).

2   Camp, "How a Common Hollywood Screenwriting Technique Can Transform Your Marketing."

3   J.K. Rowling, *Harry Potter* Paperback Boxed Set (Books 1–7) (New York, NY: Arthur A. Levine Books, 2009).

4   Aliyah Marr, *Unplug from the Matrix: The Truth Is Sometimes Stranger Than Fiction* (CreateSpace Independent Publishing Platform, 2014), 33.

5   Martin Luther King, "Speech at the Great March on Detroit," *Martin Luther King, Jr. and the Global Freedom Struggle*, June 23, 1963, http://kingencyclopedia.stanford.edu/encyclopedia/documentsentry/doc_speech_at_the_great_march_on_detroit.1.html (accessed April 18, 2017).

6   Rowling, *Harry Potter* Paperback Boxed Set; Barack Obama, "Super Tuesday, Chicago, IL," *Best Speeches of Barack Obama through His 2009 Inauguration*, February 5, 2008, http://obamaspeeches.com/E02-Barack-Obama-Super-Tuesday-Chicago-IL-February-5-2008.htm (accessed April 18, 2017).

7   Cornel West, "An Evening with Dr. Cornel West: Celebrating 25 Years of the UC Davis Cross Cultural Center," *Aggie Video*, May 30, 2015, https://video.ucdavis.edu/media/An+Evening+with+Dr.+Cornel+WestA+Celebrating+25+Years+of+the+UC+Davis+Cross+Cultural+Center/0_2i6s9nis (accessed April 18, 2017).

INDEX

Mandela, Nelson 51
marching 89–90, 92
Marr, Aliyah 164n4
Martin, Michele 48n7
Marx, Karl 32, 45, 48n1
Marxism 32
materialist 32–34, 44–45
Matrix, The 157, 160, 163, 164n4
Max, Steve 85n2
McCabe, Leila 60, 125, 130
McCalla, Jocelyn 48n7
McLaren, Peter 49n17
media viii, xiv, 22, 26, 38, 55–56, 73,
    75, 81, 87–89, 90, 92–93, 95, 97,
    101, 102, 107, 111–113, 117–122,
    124, 126–127, 144, 150–151, 153,
    154
media relations team 117, 122, 126,
    129, 143, 150
Mika, Gaia xvi
Minieri, Joan 19n1, 19n3–5, 49n11,
    69n3–7, 69n9–13, 85n1–3,
    108n1–2, 108n4–8, 109n11–14,
    141n1, 152n1
Mueller, Carol 48n7

National Association of Colored
    Women 37
negotiation xiv, 90, 100

Oakland Training Institute 42
Obama, Barack xiii, xviin1, 79, 105,
    162, 164n6
occupying spaces 96, 98–99
Occupy Movement 99
organizational rap 6, 57–60, 62, 64,
    114, 143, 150–151
organized money 53–54
organized people 53–54
organized violence 53–54
Ortiz, Lucila 68, 137

Paine, Thomas 72
Parson, Talcott 44
Peavey, Fran 141n2

Pelosi, Nancy 79–80
People Improving Communities
    through Organizing (PICO) 42,
    43, 49n14
personal problems 1
picketing 89, 90, 93
Plato vii, 27–28, 31–32, 157, 162–163
Plotkin, Wendy 49n11
power for 52–54, 56
power map xiv, 55, 71, 73, 74, 80, 82,
    84, 108, 143, 144, 150, 154
power over 52, 54
power with 52–54, 68
press release 6, 115, 118–119, 122,
    124, 126
privilege viii, 11, 16, 25, 66–68
public hearings 80, 89–90, 95–96

Qayoumi, Mohammad 123

rallying 89, 90–91
Raphael 31–32
recruitment vii, xiv, 55–60, 62, 71, 84,
    111, 119, 129, 143, 144, 150–151,
    153–154
recruitment team 57, 129
research team 72–73
Reuther, Walter 52
Rivera, Tiffany 66
Robinson, Joanne 37, 48n7
Rocky Mountain Peace Center 29n1,
    29n3, 141n3–4
Ross, Fred 41
Rowling, J.K. 164n3

Saint Mary's College of California xvi
San Francisco State University xv
San José State University i, xi, xiv, xvi,
    8, 9, 12, 63–64, 81, 123
Scarritt, James xvi
School of Athens 31
SECO (South East Community
    Organization) 40
secondary target 12, 73, 80, 84
Sen, Rinku 19n3